EDEN ACROSS THE STREET
AND OTHER FORMATIVE PLACES

EDEN ACROSS THE STREET

AND OTHER FORMATIVE PLACES

a memoir

BILL KEEN

Palmetto Publishing Group
Charleston, SC

Eden Across the Street and Other Formative Places: a Memoir
Copyright © 2020 by Bill Keen
All rights reserved

First Edition

Printed in the United States

Paperback: 978-1-64990-040-1
eBook: 978-1-64990-039-5

This memoir concerns people whose lives met with mine, some for a moment, others for a longer time. The events did occur. Each proceeds from a point in historical reality outside of myself, but some have been elaborated by my memory of wished for conclusions when I was younger and others have been bolstered by written records. The language in the dialogue is an imaginative reconstruction. I have tried to be true to the essence of what was said and the oral styles of the actual speakers. I have changed a few names.

In memory of my mother and father and my wife Sally and all the teachers who, with patience and kindness, helped me to read the books of the world.

I

EDEN ACROSS THE STREET

CHAPTER ONE

Eden Across the Street: Seeing Where I Hoped to Go

At the end of summer, 2015, my wife Sally and I returned to Washington, Pennsylvania from our annual month of the green life in Hemlock Park on Lake Damariscotta near Jefferson, Maine. That lake and the acres of woods around it are among the most restorative places I know of on this continent. Sally had experienced the wonder of Lake Damariscotta for most of her life because she spent summers there, at the Wavus Camps, from her ninth year until the end of the summer following her sophomore year of college. During that period she mastered the lore and skills relevant to living in a natural setting and becoming a leader of girls a year or two younger than she. Indeed, she learned the lessons of camp life so well and conveyed her knowledge and skill so effectively that eventually she was awarded the camp's most coveted prize, the Wavus Gold Medal.

My contact with the lake has been more recent, limited to a week or two during four or five summers while I was still teaching and, after I retired in 2000, blossoming into the month to six weeks we enjoyed each year until late September 2015, the time of Sally's last trip there. I'll never master the skills that Sally and her brother Howard picked up over many years of camp life. There's little chance I'll ever sail a boat or paddle a canoe down a moon path. But I am becoming adept at catching bass, perch and pickerel from the shore or by trolling when one of the skilled persons, my son-in-law Paul or one of his sons, Parker or Zach, mans the motor boat. And I can keep up with the best of them getting down to the Muscongus Bay Lobster Pound, where the fare will be a peck of long-necked clams, a pound-and-a-half hard-shelled lobster, a big bag of Cape Cod potato chips (anywhere else I'd eat Utz), and some ice-cold beer or white wine. I can do this gig for as long as the weather stays nice and the lobster pound stays open. Usually that's until Columbus Day.

In some years, Sally and I had to leave Maine earlier than the beginning of October because we needed to get ready for a fall trip to a faraway place with the hostile elders of Road Scholars. In 2010, for instance, we had to shut the cabin at the end of August in order to prepare for the trip we'd take to China in September and October. Sal and I arrived home for the several days we'd need to pack our travel clothes and an arsenal of drugs, the kind prescribed for old folks to keep their limbs moving, their minds more or less focusing, and their hearts from exploding.

To ensure that the supply of pills was adequate, we had to endure multiple doctors' appointments. We weren't on the green side of sixty anymore, and we wouldn't just be headed to Nag's Head. Yeah, and who wants to see dotty old Americans wandering about Tiananmen Square or passed out nose-down in the hot and sour soup? What are the chances we wouldn't have our pictures snapped, the result ending up in newspapers internationally and as a "Ha-Ha" feature on the six o'clock news? So we endured the examinations and grabbed and filled the scripts. Then we packed bags and checked lists and checked again in the best geriatric way.

Thinking we were ready, I decided on a last check of emails and discovered a new one. It was from the president of the Fortnightly Club, a local organization of folks in Washington, Pennsylvania who get together every fortnight and hurl words at one another. I'd been called on to be the speaker about once every third year since I'd joined up twenty-some years back. The email informed me that, the fates willing, I was to be the final speaker for the 2010-2011 season, the picnic meeting, which the year before had been held in Washington Park.

I have always been a lover of parks. As a city boy, I owe my early experience of the green world to parks. And the skills I picked up in and around my hometown park, though I never won a medal for my efforts, have given me fond memories and helped me appreciate the advantage my adopted home, Washpa, has in being blessed with its own wonderful park. So, when I received the email announcing my assignment, I savored the task of filling the spring air of Washington with my vocables. Since I'd have nine months to get ready, I thought I'd be able to fling something together that would keep old boys and girls full of dinner awake and amused. At the time, I didn't actually know where the picnic meeting would be held. Rain could drive us into a church basement or to Tom Hart's barn, but I liked the idea that the gathering might be in Washington Park.

The first celebration of my time as a teacher at W&J College was the September 1966 picnic in the park's stone pavilion. It was hosted by the college's president, Boyd Crumrine Patterson, and his bluestocking wife Mayno. For years after that, the picnic was held at this same place; and I, for one, always looked forward to it. What a gem Washington's city park is! You can play tennis and softball there, cross-country ski, walk the trails, or watch the upcoming generations learn how to hit and field and throw as they make their way through the levels of boys' baseball. I didn't have any sons of my own to watch speeding around the diamond, but I did get the chance to see my daughter Suzanne waltz on the park's ice rink with the onetime Olympian Michael Siebert as part of her training in the Ice and Blades Skating Club; and I applauded my daughter Rachel when she held her own in a youth soccer league dominated by adolescent boys. And I applauded my daughter Rebecca as she danced in the chorus of two summer musicals in the roaring twenties pavilion. I, too, got to perform there, in my pajamas, as a member of the chorus in another summer musical. I truly appreciate Washington Park; it has afforded me a continuation of a city kid's need for grass and trees and acres of space to roam that goes back to the days of my childhood in Wiconisco and then onWhitehall Street in Harrisburg.

My first home was in Wiconisco, a small coal-mining town at the upper end of Dauphin County. Wiconisco didn't have much in the way of parks. You could always see trees, of course, because Wiconisco is set on the side of a mountain. Maybe that's why the villagers didn't think they needed a park, or maybe the closeness of the Lykens Glen, a real park, satisfied the need for sylvan spaces. Anyhow, the closest thing to a park in Wiconisco was on Pottsville Street, where half a block of open space ran down to the new high school gymnasium my father, just out of Penn State's architecture program, had designed in 1930. A job in 1930? Connections, you know, connections. His father was a state legislator. For the Fourth of July, a temporary bandstand had been set up near the bottom of that open space, and the local tootlers, blasters, and drummers were scheduled to torture anyone who stopped to listen with their rendition of "The Stars and Stripes Forever." I was still a month or so short of four years old and still addicted to afternoon naps. Sometime before the local noisemakers began to play their tunes, I crept under the bandstand and took a nap, a longer one than usual, as it happened, and a deep enough one that I missed the whole concert.

When I awoke late in the afternoon and crawled out from under the bandstand, I was greeted by members of the fire brigade fumbling up and down Pottsville Street hollering my name. Even at less than four years of age, I knew I was about to catch hell.

A year later, the Keen family moved to 2033 Whitehall Street in Harrisburg. The front door of our new house opened to a view of Reservoir Park right across the street. I know, of course, that not all city kids agree about the wonders of nature. A colleague of mine at Oswego State and his wife hailed from Detroit, and in that small New York town the only place that satisfied their need for constant traffic in the streets and people on the sidewalks was a second-floor apartment above the only convenience store on the main street that stayed open after nine in the evening. Sally and I, on the other hand, as soon we could manage it, moved from the cramped bungalow we'd rented in Oswego to rural Dempster, where we could see trees and cows and where more than a couple of cars passing our house in a day was almost a traffic jam. Yeah, I know, it takes all kinds.

Talk about cars! We all seem to be obsessed with them; in my case it's because of the unlikeliness during World War II of traveling anywhere in a car. The Depression had already cramped the Keens' travel plans, and the war and my dad's uncertain employment history kept us stuck at the curb. Pappy did own a car, but it was almost as old as I was: the 1938 Chevrolet spent most of its time sitting in front of our house and incubating rust. When the war had been over for a couple of years, my father was still coaxing life out of the bucket of bolts that had done more than its expected hitch, enduring the shell shock of potholes but winning no Purple Hearts. Two numbers down the street, in front of the house of our neighbor, Steve Bratchler, gleamed the *second* new car since the resumption of automaking in Detroit. So much salt in our wounds!

My father never said anything directly about his frustration as he sweated to start our relic and whispered sweet nothings into its carburetor to get us down to Philadelphia for the semiannual reunion with his sister Marion, but he did allow himself to joke about any man spending half his life polishing a car only to trade it in every other year. "Maybe old Steve is being paid by Detroit to act as the local advertiser for Pontiac," he quipped. I, too, wondered about Mr. Bratchler's car, but with less humor than my father. What had we done to offend the money gods who kept laying off Pappy at the end of every job, making it necessary to continue "meatless

Tuesdays" and to fill up on an endless diet of the soybeans we'd been conned into thinking was an enjoyable substitute for meat?

My mother, always the optimist, counseled a brighter outlook. Even Truman wasn't doing as bad a job as she'd feared when he first took over at Roosevelt's death. Housing starts were on the rise, she said, and soon the veterans would want better houses than the identical little boxes springing up beyond Twenty-first and Berryhill and chewing up the fields out past Twenty-fifth and Market where we'd always been able to liberate corn to hurl at neighborhood porches on Halloween, when John Harris High and the cemetery were the last structures at the end of Market Street. She was sure that my father was bound to get on with a developer who sought to offer variety in housing to more affluent clients and would need a first-rate architect to design personalized abodes.

As it turned out, my mother was right, but it took at least another year before the developers of Country Club Hills in Camp Hill would hire my dad so her prediction could come true. In the meantime, I tried to follow her advice about counting my blessings as well as her directive to work hard in school so I could enter a better-paying profession than architecture. She favored the law for me because, before marriage, she'd dated lots of lawyers and they'd all driven new and very substantial cars. The law—maybe that would work out. I know for sure that not on the coldest day in hell or the hottest in heaven would I have studied architecture. Good grief, think of the lifelong sentence of math courses that path would require! I did try to count my blessings. At first, I had trouble getting past a couple of lame ones like not having to take tub baths when the hot water heater was busted and being able to supplement my diet with library paste at school.

"Oh, Bill," my mother said, giving me a skeptical look, "you can do better than that." Then, handing me a pencil and a page from a legal pad, she said, "fill up both sides and I'll think about baking you the blessing of a whole custard pie the next time eggs are on sale." Who said bribery was a crime? Whoever it was didn't know how good my mother's pies were.

My list was forced through several revisions because my mother vetoed as blessings the items she called products of negative thinking, such as our not being able to afford what I thought of as extracurricular tortures (elocution and dancing lessons forced on kids from better-heeled families who lived in Bellevue Park). "It's not a blessing to miss out on experiences that would do you some good," she declared. Though I muttered a protest against changing the rules after the start, I could see that these items were jeopardizing the custard pie, so I erased them from the list; but I tucked them away in my own private trove.

I can't now remember all the items I came up with that she finally approved, but prominent ones were that the U.S.

had won the war; that the Germans hadn't bombed our neighborhood as I mistakenly thought they could; that we could still afford hard beer pretzels and an occasional hunk of Lebanon bologna from the end of the roll at a discount price. I also listed Uncle Pete's contributions; he brought us lots of sweet corn and potatoes and the most delicious white freestone peaches from his truck farm outside of Penbrook. And I didn't forget that my grandmother still made potato soup and chicken corn soup with fried crumbles. I was a growing boy, and, to me, blessings were good things to eat. They still are.

Though I knew better than to put it on my list, the ease with which I had escaped from weekly piano lessons when practicing endless finger exercises began to interfere with playing basketball was another advantage of the family's being short of cash. My mother sighed, "Oh,, Bill, you have an artist's fingers," but she did let me quit the piano lessons. I think she consulted her "inner light" and concluded that the fifty cents a week she was spending to turn me into a junior Jose Iturbi could be put to better uses. I was glad she was so practical, but when I bunged one of my "artist's fingers" in the rougher sports, I kept that cost from her.

Of all the blessings I listed, the greatest, undoubtedly, was my good fortune in living right across the street from one of Harrisburg's most extensive assets, Reservoir Park. Dear hearts, if you grew up in Harrisburg sometime around the end of World War II, you probably already know as much as I do about Reservoir Park, its location, its size, its major assets, and some of its unusual features. If so, you may want to skip this passage of stats and description I'm including here because this little book may actually come under the uninformed gaze of someone unacquainted with our once fair city and its most marvelous park. Our most marvelous park, I say, because there are half a dozen others; but none can hold a candle to Reservoir Park. It earns pride of place. The others may have to wait until, on a slow day sometime in the future, I get around to them.

Reservoir Park ran six longer-than-average city blocks from Eighteenth and Walnut to Twenty-Fourth and Market on its longest side. It climbed a steady rise from Eighteenth Street to its highest point above Catholic High School, which was perched looking down on Market Street between Twenty-First and Twenty-Second. Reservoir Park had very little automobile traffic during the war, but when cars came back, that changed. As I first knew the park, it was a place where people went for walks in spring, summer, and fall, and for sled rides in the winter, all without fear of being run down by a car. It was my mother who first led me up into Reservoir Park. I could see it on my own, of course, because the southern side of it ended just across the street from 2033 Whitehall. A road started up into the park on our block and ran up to the greenhouse, where flowers and shrubs to beautify the city were being cultivated. I saw the city trucks go up that road for a load of living plants and back down with trees and shrubs and flowers. But when we first lived on Whitehall Street, I had to be content with watching others enter the park up that road, because I'd been strictly forbidden to cross the street.

Enid Parker Keen was a dynamic, creative, and very determined woman. She wanted the best for us and the best out of us. And the only way I can define what these expectations mean is by recounting the issues and the attitudes that swept into Pennsylvania from Indiana like a brisk wind when her father finally listened to her younger brother Donald. He said to his father, "Weebob has to get out of here or she will die an early death from scrubbing everyone else's floors, having the hot lead from linotype burn her legs, and remembering that she'd been offered a scholarship to art school which no one took seriously."

Weebob? No, she wasn't little, and who knows about the "bob"? My best guess is that "Weebob" was what, as a little boy, her brother Donald thought people were saying when they referred to her by her actual name, "Enid." My grandmother, Maude Billheimer Parker, was a reader of Tennyson. Had Enid been a boy, what would Donald have made of "Geraint"? It doesn't really matter. People are what you know of them as well as what you call them. "Weebob" was good enough for Uncle Donald. It was good enough for my father, who learned fast what the beautiful woman he wanted to marry was called by her closest sibling; and it's good enough for me.

Since I was her first child and, for almost five years, her only child, and my father worked what, in terms of the time it kept him away from home, amounted to two jobs, I got a lot of my mother's attention, even after June 1940, when my sister Barbara Jane was born. Maybe she thought I was a project needing a lot of work over time to turn out half decent.

My mother hated to be cooped up in a house. She had grown up in too small a house with too many other people. Throughout the year, when the sun was shining and she could talk my grandmother or Aunt Marion into babysitting Barbie, she would take my hand and announce that she and I were going for a walk. She called it a walk, but, to me, it seemed more like a run.

My mother was very athletic. As far as I know, she never ran competitively; but she certainly could have. Even in her seventies, she could maintain a wicked pace. Did schools have women's track teams in 1920? Or was Babe Didrikson one of a kind? What my mother did do competitively was swim and study—she studied so avidly that her teachers twice recommended that she skip a grade. More impressive, I think, she became a strong swimmer by churning the waters in Hawkins Pond, run by her grandfather, Charles Owen Parker. The pond sat there for my mother to use all summer long and, from the time she was thirteen, to serve as a life-guard. She competed with members of he high school swim team—her older brother Kenneth, a contender for state honors, her cousin Asa, and Francis Peacock, the young man who would eventually marry her cousin Amelia.

A story I once heard while sitting at my grandfather's table, my jug ears open to catch what the adults were saying between bouts of euchre, was that when Johnny Weissmuller, the wonderful Olympic swimmer, visited Hawkins Pond and invited locals to have a swim with him on a day when all the super young men were away (at a meet? at a war?), my mother was among those who volunteered to have a go with the man who would be Tarzan, and she was the only one who could keep up.

First in Wiconisco and then in Harrisburg, my mother and I walked—at a very brisk pace. And she tutored me in important subjects while we walked. It was remarkable that she had the breath for power walking and potent lecturing at the same time. Strong lungs from all that swimming.

One day in the spring of our second year in Harrisburg, when it was warm enough to lure people out of their houses, my mother took me by the hand and said, "Come on, Bill, let's go pick supper." She handed me an empty A&P bag. She had another one for herself.

"What do you mean, Mama? Are we going to the store?" I asked.

"Nope!"

"Are we going to Uncle Pete's farm? I heard Gramma say it's too early for his strawberries, and, anyhow, Penbrook is too far to walk."

"No, it's not too far to walk, and we'd walk there right now if his strawberries were ripe; but your Gramma is right about Uncle Pete's strawberries not being ripe, and they won't be until a couple of weeks or maybe even a month from now."

"Aw, Mama, where are we going?"

"You certainly do have a lot of questions. Do you know what my dad used to say when I pestered him about where we were going?"

"No, I don't."

"Well, do you want to know what he'd say?"

"Yeah, I guess."

"You guess? You don't know?"

"Aw, Mama. Yes, I want to know."

"Well, he'd say, 'You'll know when we get there.' And then he'd say, 'And we'd get there a lot faster if you'd ask fewer questions.'"

Yeah, you guessed it—I shut up; but I think my notion that absent relatives can be irritating dates from about that time. And I also think my mother edited her father's reply, because I'd heard her tell the same tale to my father and the questions were "damn stupid questions" that time. Maybe she should have learned to whisper when I was around.

We'd reached the upper end of Whitehall Street where it terminated in a huge flowerpot, the destination of some of those city trucks loaded with flowers that I'd watched from our front porch.

"Hold my hand, Bill. We're crossing over here, and I don't want you to get hit by a bus."

I took my mother's hand, and she led me across Whitehall and onto the street that ran up into the park. "This is Taylor Boulevard," she said, "named after M. Harvey Taylor, a very important man in Harrisburg. Your Grandpa Keen knew M. Harvey Taylor. Your grandpa was a member of the state legislature. You know that because I've told you before. M. Harvey Taylor was one of the most important members of the Republican Party in the whole county and the most important one in Harrisburg."

"Are we going to see M. Harvey Taylor?"

"No, Bill. He doesn't live on Taylor Boulevard. Joe Kline lives in that beautiful house right there," my mother said, pointing at the first house on Taylor Boulevard. Compared to our half of a double house, the place looked like a palace. Like ours, Joe Kline's house had bushes along its front, the kind that would eventually produce bunches of pink and blue flowers. My mother loved them, so she had planted two in our postage-stamp sized front yard. Joe Kline's house had eight of them.

"Joe Kline developed this street and named it after his friend, M. Harvey Taylor," my mother explained.

"Are we going to see Joe Kline?"

"No, Bill. Joe Kline wouldn't know who we were."

"Did Joe Kline know Grandpa Keen?"

"Yes, Bill, he knew your Grandpa Keen, but Grandpa Keen is dead, and Joe Kline spends his time with politicians who are still alive."

"Then why have we come up here, Mama?"

"Because it was on the way."

I didn't ask what Taylor Boulevard was on the way to. I shut my mouth and walked faster. But this way that was on the way was all uphill. I needed all my breath to get to where we were going and, maybe, to find out why we'd come.

When we reached the last house at the top of Taylor Boulevard, my mother told me we were almost at our destination. I didn't think it could be that last house on the street Joe Kline had developed to honor his friend, because my mother was looking straight ahead where the road leveled off and began to bend to the right. She quickened her pace, leaving me behind, crossed the road to its right side, and waited for me to get there.

"There it is!" she said. "Look both ways before you cross the road."

"What is it?" I asked.

"Devil's Dip, Bill; this is Devil's Dip!"

I wanted to say "So what?" in the deflating way Rennie Phillpot said it whenever I made an excited statement, but I didn't. I kept my mouth shut, and I waited. I may actually have learned something about dealing with my mother's enthusiasm on that day.

"This is a great place to pick them," she said. "They grow profusely here, and there's hardly any automobile traffic in the park these days, so they'll be purer than the driven snow."

"What are they, Mama?" I'd looked down into Devil's Dip, and all I'd thought I could see was grass.

"Why Dandelions, Bill, millions of dandelions."

"I thought dandelions were yellow flowers called damned dandelions. That's what Uncle Charles calls them when he tears them out of the backyard at 1310 State Street."

"Dandelions do develop yellow flowers eventually, Bill, but these haven't bloomed yet, so they'll be very tender. And your uncle Charles ought to watch his language."

I hoped Uncle Charles wouldn't watch his language. I loved to listen to his stories about driving a mule-drawn wagon through the South when the South was getting electricity. He had wonderful ways of describing the mules and their habits, none of which my mother would have approved of.

"Come on, Bill. Let's pick some dandelions. We need to fill both of these bags."

"Why, Mama? Are we going to sell them?"

"Well, Bill, we probably could; but we aren't going to sell them. We're going to eat them! There's a pound of bacon at home, and your Grandmother Keen is a wizard in the kitchen when there's a pound of bacon around. Just wait until you taste those dandelions when they're drowned in hot bacon dressing."

My mother had some strange ideas about what a kid would like to eat. But I kept the thought to myself and listened carefully as she explained how to pick dandelions. She handed me an old fork. "It shouldn't be too hard to pick these dandelions, because it rained last night. We shouldn't have any trouble getting them out of the ground." Then, sticking another old fork into the ground underneath a dandelion, she snapped the plant free of its root.

"Golly," I exclaimed, "when Uncle Charles leaves the root in the ground, he says lots of bad words."

"That's because Uncle Charles doesn't eat dandelions. We do, and that root will grow more for us to eat another time."

Just as she concluded her instructions, an old man who was being pulled along by a massive bulldog stumbled into Devil's Dip. The bulldog sniffed out a prime spot, lifted a leg, and released a sizzling yellow stream.

My mother directed my attention to the busy dog. "We won't pick dandelions from over there."

"You mean where the dog just pissed?"

"Did his business, Bill," my mother whispered in the way she would when we were in church or a department store and she wanted to control my behavior without others knowing what she was doing. It was a whisper for sure, but it was full of something that stung. "Who taught you *that* word? Was it Uncle Charles? I'm going to have to talk to him about his language!"

"No, Mama, it was Joe Fiedler. He always teaches me the real words for things people do and say."

After that, my mother did no more whispering in her "on the warpath way," as my dad called it, and we picked dandelions in silence, avoiding that area where the bulldog had done his business. Soon the bags were full. I wondered how my mother knew that no other dogs had done their business in the areas we had taken dandelions from, but I thought I'd better not ask. But I would make sure those dandelions got a thorough scrubbing before they hit the pot.

Then, our picking mission completed, mother said, "C'mon, Bill, I want to show you something else. Leave the bags here; we'll pick them up on the way back." She grabbed my hand and led me up the side of Devil's Dip and across the road. We climbed up some more hillside, and just when I was getting ready to complain, she said, "There it is!" Ahead of us and up still more hillside was a statue of a big animal.

"That's the Elk," she announced, "and when we get to it, you can take a ride on its back."

"Why is it here, Mama?"

"It's here because there's a men's club called the Elks in Harrisburg, and lots of other places, too. Your Uncle Charles belongs to it."

"Why do the men need a club, Mama?"

"Lots of reasons, Bill; but that's a story for another time."

"Why does Uncle Charles need a club? Should I ask him?"

"No, Bill, don't ask him; probably it's because he lives with Aunt Alice and Aunt Cora."

We reached the elk and my mother lifted me up for a ride on its back. I looked out over the winding road of the park and thought there was a lot more to this place than Devil's Dip.

When I was on my feet again, I said, "That was fun, Mama; I'm glad Uncle Charles and the other men needed a club!"

When we'd reclaimed our bags full of dandelions, my mother said we'd take the shortcut home. Taking my hand, she led me back in the direction of the last house on Taylor Boulevard. Just short of it, she turned right onto a path that led downhill toward the greenhouse and tugged me along until we reached the the road the city trucks drove up to be loaded down with shrubs and flowers.

"So that's where it goes," I said to myself, toting my bag full of dandelions and wondering how good the hot bacon dressing would have to be to make me forget that other creatures than the bulldog my mother and I had seen made regular visits to Devil's Dip.

I was glad to see that Grandma Keen cleaned the daylights out of those dandelions. She was a Methodist and knew that anything mundane was likely to be dirty. No, back then I didn't know what "mundane" meant; but I'd had more than enough lessons from more than enough relatives about how much of life in the world was dirty.

Years later, when my wife Sally and I and our three daughters were living in Washington, Pennsylvania, early spring showers followed by uncharacteristic sunshine brought me out into the backyard on a Saturday morning. I discovered a profusion of dandelions. The yard was fifty feet wide and ran for a hundred and fifty feet behind the house. I'd paid Nathan Hamilton, my handyman, to erect an eight-foot fence around the upper third of the yard to protect my salad garden and Sally's annual blossoms from the deer that romped around East Washington. In about half of the protected area, grass was the only occupant—until the dandelions appeared.

"By God," I said to myself, "I'm going to pick those dandelions. That would make my mother proud!" Why not? Neither dogs nor deer nor groundhogs had gotten into that space since Nathan had raised the noble fence. The interstate highways were almost a mile away, and the prevailing wind visited my place first, then licked its way up to the intersection of I-70 and I-79.

By this time—the early 1980s—my Grandmother Keen had died, so I called my mother, who was living in New Jersey with Brother Jim and his wife Cheryl. My mother claimed she didn't know the recipe.

"Making hot dressing for dandelions was Gramma Keen's job; she was a wizard whenever there was a pound of bacon in the fridge. Use your imagination, Bill; that's what the PA. Dutch would do."

"PA. Dutch," I said to myself. "Why didn't I think of that?" I thanked my mother, hung up the phone, and began a whole-house search for the old Pennsylvania Dutch cookbook I knew was lurking in some dark cupboard.

Imagination is good, but the accumulated experience of PA. Dutch cooks is way better. After half an hour's search, I found my copy of *The New Pennsylvania Dutch Cookbook*, edited by Ruth Hutchison and published by Harper in 1958. In the rich lawn of the index, "Dandelion Greens" popped up. The recipes were almost as numerous as the fresh young plants basking in early spring sunshine in my backyard.

"C'mon, girls," I hollered, "we've got a job to do."

Suzanne retorted that she had to go to the library to return books; then she was going to read all day long and check out new ones.

"Better take a sandwich," I said.

Rebecca was nowhere to be found; probably she was up at Hilary Fitch's house on the top of the town. At the sound of my voice announcing a cooperative venture, Rachel had fled to the toilet. Sally was taking a nap. We'd been out late at a faculty party the night before.

"Never mind," I said to myself, "I'll do it." And I did it. I picked every volunteer that had had the good sense to spring up in the protected area of my yard, and I communed all the while with my Pennsylvania Dutch ancestors. It was better than going to church. When my shopping bags were full, I went into the kitchen and, following the instructions of Mrs. Thomas B. Keck, I washed the plants and shook them dry. The yield was well over a pound, so I fiddled with the recipe. Here it is.

Dandelion Greens
Dandelion greens
4 slices of bacon
Dressing
2 tablespoons bacon fat
1 egg yolk
3 tablespoons vinegar
1 teaspoon flour
2 tablespoons sour cream
1/2 teaspoon salt
1 teaspoon sugar

Fry the bacon, remove from pan, and crumble. Drain off bacon fat from pan, return 2 tablespoons. Add vinegar and sour cream to fat. Add a little water to egg yolk and blend with flour. Stir into the mixture in the pan over low heat, stirring constantly as dressing thickens. Add salt and sugar. Bring to a quick boil and pour over greens at once. Scatter bacon on top.

Sally must have smelled the bacon cooking, because there she was, arisen from her nap and smiling. Suzanne was still at the library. Rebecca was still at Hilary's. Rachel had vacated the toilet and had fled to the third floor, where she was playing one of my Beatles records and singing off key. It was only midafternoon by then, but Sally and I ate the dandelions with hot bacon dressing. Yum!

CHAPTER TWO

Down by the Riverside:
Hearing We Might Have to Move Again

During the summer of my introduction to dandelions, my mother took me for walks on several occasions, usually after we'd been cooped up in the house during a rainy spell. My father was always at work all day long and sometimes on the weekends too; so my mother was my usual companion, the one who fed my dreams by telling me where one day we might go, and actually taking me to places close enough to walk to. There was hardly ever another boy my age around to play with. At my house, Mama, not Papa, was all.

In September 1941, soon after my sixth birthday, I had entered the first grade at Forney School, virtually my first opportunity to learn how to deal with other kids. I suspect the delay in my socialization wasn't unusual. In those days, public school started with first grade. I don't remember ever hearing of nursery school or day care. The preparation I received was dished out by my mother. Very often, it took place on a walk which she initiated by taking my hand and dragging me along behind her. My mother had long legs and, as I've said before, she could move.

With the start of school, I hadn't been as available for spur of the moment hikes, except on the weekends; so she'd been walking by herself, and later, while I ate a post school cookie and drank a glass of milk, she'd tell me where she'd gone ("Over to 1310 State Street to see Uncle Charles and Aunt Alice"), what she'd seen along the way ("Whistlers are painting the trim on their house again and it doesn't need it"), and naming anyone she'd met along the way and saying what they'd talked about ("Mrs. Fiedler says her son Joe doesn't like school"). I already knew that Joe Fiedler didn't like school. Joe, a classmate in Miss Ensminger's first grade, had quickly established himself as the spokesman for us all, proclaiming in a loud voice that school was like jail. Miss Ensminger had frowned at Joe and shook her finger at him to make him stop.

My mother's walks became less frequent once the weather turned cold and the snow came down. It was a long winter with a lot of snow. When spring of 1942 finally arrived and brought with it a sunny Saturday, and my father was sleeping late because he hadn't come home from work the night before until I was already in bed, my mother said to me, "Come on, Bill, we've got to get out of this house. The sun is shining, and the birds are singing." Then, in a louder voice, sweetened with something artificial, she cajoled my aunt into caring for Barbie while she and I walked downtown to return our library books. *The Little Engine That Could* or some other classic of character-building propaganda had done its thing and needed to return to the roundhouse. That meant my mother and I would be walking all the way downtown, almost to the river. I knew the way: we'd done it before. We'd follow Ethel Alley to Twentieth Street, do a half a block down Twentieth to Market and then hike eighteen blocks down Market Street to the square at Second Street. Fortunately, the walking was either downhill or on the level.

Sometimes, we'd start out that same way but turn right at the corner just beyond the subway, the underpass above which the trains heading north upriver would rumble over us. At the corner beyond the subway stood Greenberg's Army and Navy Store, where, later on, I'd be suited up in war surplus gear at an affordable price. My Quaker mother might not have approved of guns and armies, but her desire for bargains, bred in the Great Depression, caused her to look the other way as I was provided with khakis and combat boots. Before a stop at Greenberg's for bargains came into play, when we took the turn to the right, we'd walk over to Capital Park, sit on a bench, and feed peanuts to the squirrels. I'd eat as many peanuts as I dispensed. Then we'd go back to Market Street, stroll by the important stores—Bowman's, Doutrich's, and Pomeroy's, stopping occasionally to look in the windows so my mother could scope out sales.

When she'd first come to Harrisburg, she told me, she'd worked at both Bowman's and Pomeroy's; and at one of those long-gone stores, had been stationed in front of cages filled with canaries and told to talk to them until they started to sing. It sounded improbable to me; but that's what my mother told me. Do you think a pious Quaker girl from Indiana would stuff her son full of fibs? While we strolled through the heart of downtown Harrisburg, I'd take notice of the movie theaters—Loews Regent and the Colonial on Market Street and the Senate around the corner at Second Street on the square. After a couple of trips, when I'd developed some minimal reading skills, I got the idea to memorize the shows playing at each theater and make it my responsibility to inform my father of the offerings that evening at suppertime—in case he was flush and thought one of the shows sounded educationally broadening. His bar for cultural value was considerably lower than my mother's and included cowboy movies as introductions to the history and geography of a part of the U.S. that none of us had ever visited.

Also, while we were on the square, my mother would ask me if I had to do *number one* or *number two.* If I did, she would take me by the hand and lead me down a flight of stairs to the public toilet, embarrassing me by taking me into the women's side. On the rare occasion when my father was along, I'd go with him into the men's side and stand at a urinal to pee, which, as everyone knows, is the real name of *Number One.*

This duty done, we'd rise from the depths and make our way to Walnut Street and the library. I'd return my books and find new ones to check out. My choices would have to meet my mother's approval: no war stories, no violent encounters or guns of any kind. Such fare was too much like the ubiquitous Action Comics she heartily disapproved of. As I've said, she was a Quaker.

Our books returned and new ones checked out, ordinarily we'd leave the library and head back the way we'd come; but before reaching the square, we'd enter Davenport's Restaurant for hot roast beef sandwiches and mashed potatoes and gravy. We'd drink water so that the lunches would cost only twenty-five cents apiece. Then we'd walk to the bus area on the square and catch the Number 2 bus, saving us the walk home that, from Cameron Street on, was almost entirely uphill. It was worth the seven-cent fare. Not bad—to downtown and back on under a dollar. A Quaker knows how to pinch a dime until it squeals.

On that day early in the summer when I was six going on seven, when we exited the library and I was already tasting a hot roast beef sandwich at Davenport's, my mother changed the game. Taking my hand, she redirected me away from the hot roast beef that was steaming in my imagination and led

me toward Front Street and across it to the green strip between the road and the river.

"Where're we going?" I whined.

"Down this way to a spot in the shade," she said.

We walked for a block until my mother found a shaded
spot she approved of and we sat on the soft grass beneath
a spreading chestnut tree. At least, I thought it must be a
chestnut tree, because my mother began to recite, "Under a
spreading chestnut tree the village smithy stands." I guess I
must have looked bewildered, because my mother laughed
and told me to sit down. "Only a poem, Bill; maybe someday you'll learn to recite poetry, too." As improbable as that
prediction must have seemed to me at the time, I eventually
did learn to recite poems, and to write them, too. If she were
still here, I'd say, "Thanks, Mama, for the poems."

"This," she said, pointing up and down the green strip
that extended further in each direction than I could see, "is
River Front Park. And that," she added, pointing at a big
house across the street, "is John Harris's mansion. You know
who John Harris was, don't you, Bill?"

"Yeah," I answered, fearing the onset of another of the
history lessons which both of my parents reveled in. Usually
my father's dutchy dissertations were ignited by a historical marker; you saw the marker and you battened down the
hatches. But I never knew what would stimulate my mother
into a history lecture. Her associations and reactions were

much too complex for a kid to figure out. I just had to look attentive and hope the lesson wasn't a long one.

The history of all the developments that followed from John Harris's settling in the Susquehanna Valley could have been a very long story, but that afternoon my mother stuck to basic elements of the early days—John Harris's establishing a trading post and a ferry across the river and his almost being burned by hostile Indians who'd been drinking *big people's naughty juice.* A few years earlier, when my mother had used this euphemism, I'd wondered what it meant, but I only had to use the phrase once at school to find out from my classmates that the beverage's real name was *whiskey.*

When she thought I'd been instructed sufficiently in the history of our city's founder, she said, "I know this has been a lot to take in, Bill, but since you'll probably be going to John Harris High School someday if we stay here in Harrisburg. . ." cutting herself short but not quickly enough to curtail the tease. I remember sitting silent for longer than was usual for a boy full of questions. We'd already moved once, leaving all that was familiar behind in Wiconisco, particularly the old store full of neat stuff where I was free to roam and summer picnics at the Glen in Lykens.

Since our first months in Harrisburg had been during the summer, I had barely met any kids my own age. When fall finally arrived and my mother marched me to Forney School to enter me in the first grade, I'd been elated to see boys my own age. By the end of that first year, I'd begun to make what I thought would be my lifelong friends, Joe Fiedler and Donnie Chornak for sure. I didn't want to lose them. Making friends had been hard work for a kid who'd spent most of his short life without boys his own age to play with, and I'd worked hard to develop just a couple in my first year of school.

"We're not going to move again, are we?"

My mother must have sensed my trepidation, because she assumed her most positive manner. "Don't worry, Bill, you'll be here a long time, and I'll probably be as old as your grandmother before I live anywhere else." With that, my mother stood up. "Let's get our legs a-moving," she said. "I've kept you here too long, and we need to get to Davenport's."

"Won't that make you late getting home to cook supper? Won't Daddy be upset?"

"Don't worry about it, Bill; he'll get over it. I'll bake a cake tomorrow. Besides, I've got a nickel for the pay phone at Kaplan's. Your Aunt Marion can fix supper."

"She won't make those little sandwiches without any crust, will she? That would really upset him," I proclaimed, adding in thought only, *and me too.*

"I'll tell her not to. Your Aunt Marion has a master's degree in home economics. I'm sure she knows how to fry chicken."

"Fried chicken, oh, boy. And can we have brown coats too?"

"I'll suggest it, but that's a lot of frying for our little stove. Maybe you'll have to wait until tomorrow for the brown coats. Besides, I'm the potato fryer; your grandmother Keen taught me the Pennsylvania Dutch way. Neither of us has a master's degree."

Fried chicken would be good, and brown coats tomorrow, and cake too. Maybe my dad would invest in some vanilla ice cream. I smiled the whole way to Davenport's, reminding myself to always sit patiently when one of my parents was delivering improving lectures that might make us late for dinner and lead to improved offerings.

For a couple of days, I put that trip with my mother to River Front Park out of my mind. But long summer afternoons with no excitement provided by other kids leaping around to engage a boy in games can lure even a seven-year-old to fret about the holes in things. What my mother had said about leaving, and then about staying, and then about her being as old as my grandmother kept coming back to me as I hid out in my room day after day wishing school would begin again and fill up my mind with the important things that the adults of the world said I should be thinking about.

I thought about the friends I had made at Forney, Donnie Chornak and Joe Fiedler. Donnie had selected me as a straight man who would follow him around and help him pull off one of his acts. That was OK with me. He could blaze the way, and I'd do my best as a bit player.

Joe Fiedler had the opposite effect. He was a promoter of other people's talents. He had a witty tongue, and even in Miss Ensminger's first grade class he knew how to say things that would lure the kids' attention off the lessons. For each new word we encountered that Miss Ensminger wrote on the blackboard, Joe would supply a funny definition. She wrote *backyard*; Joe whispered (or thought he whispered) "Home of crab grass and garbage cans."

After a couple of these contributions, which she certainly could hear, Joe was sitting in a corner of the room as a punishment. After that, he tried to push me forward to take his place; but I was too slow on the uptake to be an adequate substitute. More to my liking were the times he loudly announced to the playground at recess that I was the fastest runner or the best marble player. Whether these broadcasts were true or not, they gave me a reputation to live up to. When you haven't made many friends and you're already six years old, it hurts to think you are going to move and start all over again. That Donny and Joe included me in any way lifted my spirits; that I might lose them cast me down in the dumps.

To turn my mind from the brooding tendency that adults—particularly Aunt Marion—had cautioned me about, I'd been working on an airplane made of balsa wood, gluing pieces together to form the structures of its wings. I'd waited long enough, I thought, for the glue to hold; but when I picked up one wing, its joints slipped apart. And I knew the hole was still there in the middle of my memory about a conversation whose ends seemed further from my reach than the limits of River Front Park and entirely beyond my capacity to hold them together.

CHAPTER THREE

Houses and Roses: My Mother Dreaming

For the next four days I kept to my room even though it was sunny and the voices of little children playing in the back-yard next door came through the open window of my bedroom in excited bursts of laughter and annoyance. (Someone was teasing someone else and someone else didn't like it.) I incubated my thoughts and drained off the darker vapors by building a fantastical village from Tinkertoys, Lincoln Logs, and Kraft Cheese boxes on the floor of my bedroom, keeping uncluttered only enough space to maneuver among my growing neighborhoods and to get in and out of my bed. I left my room only for meals.

At lunch on the fourth day, my mother began to interrogate me: "What've you been doing, Bill? Why've you been staying indoors all day when the weather outside is so glorious? You know, school starts soon, and then you'll have to be inside for hours at a time. Why not get some sunshine while you can?"

"I'm building a village, and I don't want to go outside where there's no boys my age to play with."

"Right, Bill, I can see that. Why not come outside with me?" she said, getting up from the table and clearing the dishes. "Marion, would you watch Barbie?" Not waiting for an answer, she freed Barbie from her high chair and directed her toddling toward the living room, where she lifted her into the playpen. Aunt Marion followed them out of the kitchen.

"Just let me wash these dishes, Bill; then I'll take you to see a beautiful place that's close by, right here in Harrisburg."

This will take a while, I thought, but she surprised me by doing the job with unusual speed.

"OK, Bill, let's go," she chirped, flipping her apron over a chair's back and grabbing my hand. Through the living room we went, out the front door, passing on the way the penned-up Barbie and Aunt Marion in my dad's chair, reading a magazine. Then across the porch to the sidewalk she jerked me so hastily that we might have been mother and child fleeing the Johnstown flood. Up Whitehall Street toward the flowerpot at Twenty-First we galloped.

"Are we...digging...dandelions...again? Don't we need shopping bags and forks?"

"Nope, too late in the year to gather dandelions. All we need are our eyes and our noses, and maybe our ears."

At the end of the street, we turned not toward Taylor Boulevard but toward Market Street. We looked both ways and waited and waited while cars sped up and down that major thoroughfare. At last there was a break in the traffic, and my mother, with me in tow, sprinted across. On the other side, she stopped and swept her arm, with pointing finger extended, from Market Street to Twenty-First. "This is Bellevue Park," she said, "and this is where we'll live when your daddy lands a big job!"

"Could I still go to Forney?"

"Yep! You'd still go to Forney, or Edison, or John Harris, depending on how long it takes for a big contractor to recognize your daddy's talents. We'd move, but not away from your friends. Bobby Williams goes to Forney, and he lives in Bellevue Park."

"Oh, boy," I said when I'd finally caught my breath.

"Now, let me show you a wonderful spot and tell you about your Grandpa Parker."

She led me along the street that entered Bellevue Park, crossed to the other side, and stopped at a gated entranceway in a hedged lot. We went in. It was a garden full of roses. I thought I might have a sneezing fit, but my mother seemed unconcerned, because she said, "Look around, Bill, and smell the wonderful aroma. This is Mr. McFarland's garden. He's an important man who owns a publishing company, and this is his estate, Breeze Hill."

"Won't Mr. McFarland mind if we come into his garden? You always yell at kids when they come into our garden."

"No, he won't mind. The gate isn't locked. Mr. McFarland wants people to admire his garden. And I only yelled at Donnie Maxwell because he was tramping on my flowers while searching for grasshoppers."

"It sure is a big garden. It sure has a lot of roses. But where are the dandelions? Your little garden has roses *and* dandelions."

"Mr. McFarland is a purist. He specializes in roses, and he probably thinks dandelions are weeds."

"Just like Uncle Charles. Uncle Charles calls them damn…"

"Bill! Language!"

"I'm sorry, Mama. It slipped."

"Well, please don't let it slip again."

"Does Mr. McFarland know Uncle Charles?"

"I'm sure he doesn't."

"Isn't Mr. McFarland an Elk? I thought all important men were in Uncle Charles's club."

"There are other clubs, Bill—even some Uncle Charles couldn't join."

"Why couldn't Uncle Charles join those clubs?"

"Never mind, Bill; look at the roses, smell the roses, but don't pick any of them. Mr. McFarland wants them to still be here for other people to see when we've gone home."

"Do I have to smell them? I might sneeze."

"Then look twice as hard."

"OK. What are you going to tell me about Grandpa Parker? You said you were going to tell…"

"Yes, Bill; I did. When my dad got me a ticket to come to Harrisburg, he told me about lots of places I ought to visit in the city. One of them was McFarland's Gardens."

"Does Grandpa Parker know Mr. McFarland?"

"No, Bill, he doesn't; but he knows *about* Mr. McFarland. You see, your Grandpa Parker is a rose grower."

"I thought he worked on the railroad."

"He does work on the railroad; but his hobby is growing roses—he's passionate about roses. Your grandpa has even developed his own rose that may be named after him."

"Gee, I have two important grandpas."

"You certainly do. And Grandpa Parker is coming to visit us, and he'll bring Great-Grandpa Parker with him. They both love roses, and they're going to visit Mr. McFarland's garden."

"I'm going to sneeze, Mama."

"Cover your nose!"

As we left Mr. McFarland's garden, my sneezing subsided.

We walked further into Bellevue Park, my mother pointing to one big house after another and naming the important families that lived in them. I've forgotten most of the names by now, but I do remember that one of the mansions belonged to the Hershey family, owners of the Hershey ice cream plant in Harrisburg. Such folks are worth remembering.

"How do you know the people who live in all these houses, Mama?"

"I don't know them, but Isabel Whistler does, and she and
I have walked out here occasionally while you were in school."

Bellevue Park is hilly, and its roads wind their way among
the hills, adding to the distance between point A and point
B. We took a shortcut from a higher road to a lower one by
walking down a long brick staircase. It was easy going, but
I knew it would be harder going on the way back. When I
expressed my concern to my mother, she said, "Oh, Bill, you
should have been born in Kansas."

I didn't ask why, but I tucked the question away for another conversation on another day.

At the bottom of the walkway, we were at the lowest level of Bellevue Park. I spied a fair to middling pond. As we
walked by, I spotted a second pond, about the same size as
the first.

"Oh, boy, Mama; can I wade in the ponds?"

"No, Bill. I don't know how deep they are."

"Can I fish in them? Daddy said he'd take me fishing, but
he's always working. You could bring me out here to fish."

"I don't think there are any fish in them. I've never seen
anyone fishing here."

"Ah, sh—uh, shucks."

"Careful, Bill. Language."

"Yes, Mama, I know."

"Knowing is good; remembering is better. Bobby Williams from your class at Forney lives up there." She pointed up a terraced hillside to a brick house with sloping roofs. "And behind those trees is the Williamses' swimming pool. Maybe someday you'll be invited to go swimming there. I know Edna Williams; we're both in the PTA for your school."

"Oh, boy, that would be fun!"

"Well, then, try not to get in a fight with Bobbie Williams."

How did she know that Joe Fiedler had decided to be Forney's fight promoter and that he'd drafted me as his Joe Palooka? Was it some kind of magic my mother possessed, or were all mothers able to read their sons' minds? But all I said was, "So I'll get to go swimming?"

"That's right, Bill." Quakers are always trying to keep you from the rougher pleasures in life.

We walked on. I gazed at one big house after another in this woodland paradise. None of them had a second house attached. We didn't turn around to head back to the intimidating brick stairs but climbed a more modest incline toward Market Street—at least I thought it was Market Street because I heard lots of cars just out of sight ahead of us. When we reached the top of the road, my mother confirmed my guess: "See, Bill, we're back to Market Street. That wasn't so hard, was it? Just a little bit more and it will be all downhill back to our house. Two blocks the other way is John Harris, where you'll go to school someday."

Oh, thank goodness, I thought, *we're not going to move again.*

My mother interrupted any further thought about where I'd be living. "C'mon, Bill, let's cross over here."

"Why, Mama?"

"Because that's the Parkview Apartments across Market Street."

"Why do we want to go to the Parkview Apartments, Mama? Do we know someone who lives there? Do the kids who live there go to Forney?"

"Probably we do, and yes, the kids that live there would usually go to Forney; but we're crossing here because there's a soda fountain on the ground floor of the Parkview Apartments. I'm thirsty for a fountain Coke after all the walking we've done. How about you, Bill?"

"Yeah, Mama! Do they have Cloverdale Punch?"

"Well, let's go and find out."

And as we crossed over I thought to myself that walking and talking makes adults thirsty, and that's a good thing.

CHAPTER FOUR

An Expedition to Wildwood: Fishing for the Values

Harrisburg was a big city in my youth—a lot of square miles and a population of somewhat more than 83,000 when my family moved there from tiny Wiconisco in 1940. If you hailed from Philly or Pittsburgh, you might say, as I often heard, "Hell, that ain't big; that shrimp shouldn't even be the capital, 'cept it's sorta close to the center." But it seemed huge to a little kid who, with his mother, had taken morning walks around the two or three streets of Wiconisco and arrived back at the Keen house on Pottsville Street in plenty of time for lunch. In addition, Harrisburg's population wouldn't sit still in those days, climbing well over 90,000 as jobs in steel, war products manufacturing, and the various levels of government lured people from farms in the state and also from down south.

Unless some fractious borough has seceded without my hearing about it, the city's area is the same as it was back then, even though where the city's area ends might now be hard to visualize because some of the green stretches of farmland that used to spread out from just beyond Harrisburg's northern, southern, and eastern borders have been developed into sprawling suburbs that obscure the demarcations we used to be able to see. Now these suburbs house the ongoing families whose grandparents and, in some cases, great-and even great-great grandparents, used to live in the capital city.

A place as populated as Harrisburg once needed lots of park space to sooth the muscles and minds of its citizens when most of the men put in long hours in steel mills or doing the drone work of clerkdom for engineering firms, retail businesses, and the State, while the women herded large families of house apes or got themselves employed as waitresses, cashiers, and secretaries. The old Harrisburg's park system met the needs of its hardworking and steadily growing population for weekend picnics followed by snoozes for the overstuffed who would spread out on blankets and shade themselves from daylight by tenting sections of the Sunday paper over their faces. I'm sure you've gathered that Bellevue Park wasn't a place where the workers of the world would lounge on a summer Sunday; but, in addition to Reservoir Park and River Front Park, both open to democratic relaxation, there were several other green spaces for folks to visit for recreation and entertainment.

Families could go uptown to Italian Lake. But if you lived out on Allison Hill, as we did, your family had better have a car and enough gas or be willing to tote picnic baskets on a long bus ride to get there. Italian Lake had a formal feeling that didn't appeal to me. Was it the fake Oriental bridge and the manicured look? I don't remember any unruly woods where you could run around whooping and trying not to fall on your ass. Every summer the Optimist Club would sponsor a fishing tournament for kids at Italian Lake. I participated for a couple of years. A few contestants caught small goldfish, and the optimists made a big deal out of these minute accomplishments. I guess their club required them to react positively, since they were stuck with the optimist label. I didn't catch anything, and it seemed to me that, if the total catch of the day were cleaned and fried, you still wouldn't have enough fish for a decent-sized sandwich.

Further out near the northern edge of the city was Wildwood Park. My dad took me there to fish once, and we caught some fingerling trout too small to keep, but fish at any rate, and caught by us! He said we'd come back another weekend. I waited and waited. My dad worked and worked.

On a summer afternoon when I was lollygagging around Allison Hill after delivering my papers, I saw a guy who was in my grade at Edison. His name was Sweeney, and he was a year or so older than the rest of us because he'd played hooky a lot and more than once been put back a grade. He might have been scorned by the school principal and some of the teachers, but his free-spiritedness had gained him respect from me and a couple of other readers who had tackled *Huckleberry Finn* when the rest of the class had quit with Mark Twain after *Tom Sawyer.* Who says fiction doesn't apply to life?

Sweeney lived in the *projects,* which some people from Whitehall Street, including one who lived in the same house I did, looked down on, just as some people in Bellevue Park sneered at our street of nearly lawnless double houses, thus offending one who lived in the same double house that I did. It's an old story.

When I spotted Sweeney, he was pumping his bike up the considerable rise of Market Street from Cameron to Thirteenth and looking like he'd been at it for quite a while. Seeing me, he stopped to rest and to shoot the breeze. His fishing rod was strapped across the handlebars and a stringer loaded with good-sized fish hung down to the right. The catch bumped his knee on that side, making the job of getting up the hill all the harder.

"Where'd you catch them?"

"Up at Wildwood."

"Boy, I'd like to go there, too, and my dad's promised to take me, but he's been getting a lot of overtime this summer and isn't around to drive up there."

"Ya got a bike, ain't ya?" Sweeney asked. "I'm goin' back Sunday morning. Ya can come along."

I was excited by the offer.

"OK, man, meet me at Joe Bihl's over on State Street at five in the morning," he said, explaining, "Ya know, we need to get there while them fish is still huntin' fer breakfast. Gotta go, man; da fish is starting to stink," he added, and began to make much better time along the levelness of South Thirteenth Street.

"Right, see ya then," I hollered after him. In fact, I didn't have a bike or a stringer, and I'd never caught any fish large enough to keep; but it was only Wednesday, meaning I had time to talk one of my buddies into lending me a bike, probably by paying his way into the Penway for a Randolph Scott or John Wayne flick. The stringer of fish Sweeney had been toting was a powerful lure, and almost as strong was the prospect of missing Sunday school, where I'd have to attend a class led by one of the boring teachers I'd endured all week long back in grade school. When I brought up the fishing trip at supper that evening, I fabricated the group going as a bunch of guys from my class and crossed my fingers under the table that my mother wouldn't ask for names, as was her wont. Miraculously, she didn't, objecting rather, "Oh, Bill, it's so far, even if you take the bus partway, and besides, you'll miss Sunday school." What'd I tell you?

Just then, my father curtailed his holy communion with the tuna salad and leapt to my defense: "For cryin' out loud, Enid, let the boy go fishin'. A day in the woods will do him as much good as Sunday school. Hell, I wish I could go too."

Hooray, Pappy, I thought. I'd just about let my tongue slip into accusation mode—that my mother often slept in on Sunday mornings and missed Reverend Billman's sermons—but such a comment would have canned the fishing trip and most probably have cost me some other privilege too. Pappy gave me bus fare, which I accepted without explaining that I was borrowing a bike for the trip. I wasn't sure that arrangement would have his support. And I was afraid that a discussion along those lines would work back to issues my mother, thus far, had neglected to bring up. I just hoped my father was right about the spiritual power of the woods; maybe it would be strong enough to repair the damage done by my sin of omission. I'd have to keep my eye peeled for a good deed I might do to urge redemption along.

Early Sunday morning I brought out of hiding under the back porch the bike I'd borrowed from the Potter brothers for *two* admission charges to the Penway Theater. When I arrived at Joe Bihl's, I found Sweeney waiting for me. In imitation of his strategy, I'd strapped my fishing pole across the handlebars. Fortuitously, the Potter bike had a basket into which I'd put my other gear and my brown bag lunch. I told Sweeney he could put his gear in the basket.

"I ain't got no gear," he said. "All I need's a pole an' a stringa." I looked around but failed to see a brown paper bag.

"Where's your lunch?" I asked.

"I ain't brought none. I'll eat latah. Gotta catch suppah firs."

I began to understand that our reasons for going fishing weren't quite the same.

After an hour's bike ride in the blessedly cool morning, we arrived at Wildwood, and, as far as I could tell, we had the place to ourselves. *Neat-o*, I thought, *no one except Sweeney to see me if I screw up while casting*—not my strong point, because I hadn't had enough practice. As it turned out, I did pretty well, only once hooking a low-hanging branch. We fished all morning, moving from one place to another. Early on, we'd found a spot where the fish were very hungry, as Sweeney had said they would be when he'd required our early arrival. I got seven fingerlings and then a keeper catfish. What a thrill. The catfish took my line for a ride.

"Keep yer rod up or ya'll lose 'im," Sweeney advised.

I did as I had been instructed—brought my fish to the edge and eased the fighting fellow onto the bank.

"Looks like about nine inches ta me; put 'im on the stringah," Sweeney said.

By eleven o'clock, I was hungry, having eaten only a piece of toast that morning. I offered Sweeney half my sandwich, but he refused. In the true spirit of fishing, I changed the lure and held out two beer pretzels. He took them in a shot and immediately chomped away on one of them.

"Ah, them beer pretzels is good; only thing is, we ain't got no cold Schmidts to go wid 'em."

I was surprised and wondered whether he was joking. I was only thirteen, and my illicit beer-drinking in Reservoir Park was still several years in the future. Maybe Sweeney thought I didn't believe he was already a beer drinker, because he added, "I ain't bullshittin' ya; my old man always gives me some when he brings quarts home on a weekend. He says beer'll put hair on yer chest, but it ain't worked yet, not like wid them Eyetalian guys."

We continued to fish until after three in the afternoon.

"It's gettin' late," Sweeney said, "but I hate to go widout a full stringah. I got room for one more, and one a' them is yours. My old man'll be pissed. I'm doing one more cast."

He cast and almost immediately got a strong hit. The fish bent his pole. But Sweeney stuck with it, keeping the big catfish away from half-submerged brush on the far bank where it might have wound the line around a branch and broken free. He patiently worked the big fish toward him and finally docked it in the shallow water near the stream's edge. Still, the fish wasn't quitting: it tugged and twisted and worked the water into excited life.

"Take a holta the rod, Bill; keep the rod head up," Sweeney commanded me, handing me his rod. "I ain't got a net and I ain't taking the chance of losin' him by tryin' a jerk him out."

I held the rod steady while Sweeney knelt by the stream's edge.

"Lift the rod easy, Bill, so the cat's head's just outta the water." I did and Sweeney grabbed the long fish body with both hands and hefted it onto the bank. The fish squirmed fiercely, but Sweeney held on like a linebacker stopping a running back on the one. "Bad luck, Cat Man; yez is goin' home wit' me, all fifteen inches," he said, smiling up at me as he cradled the great catch to his chest.

"How 'bout that, Bill?" he said.

I sensed my chance to balance the books with the powers above: "Hey, Sweeney, you can have mine too."

"Whatta ya mean, man? He'll make a good fish sammich."

I was sure he would, and the thought of it started the juices flowing. "Yeah, but I don't like fish sandwiches much," I lied.

"Well, if ya ain't shittin' me, I'll take 'im—makes a full load ona stringah."

"Yeah," I said, "seems like that's where he ought to be."

But I wasn't entirely satisfied by the accomplished charity. True, it had felt great helping Sweeney land the big fish; and being able to contribute to his full stringer wasn't bad either; but telling a lie to get the deed done made it feel like splitting a doubleheader.

CHAPTER FIVE

Quaker Meeting in the Kitchen: A Lesson on Watching My Language

The kitchen in our house in Wiconisco may not have been as large as it seemed to me as a little kid. Being not quite five when we left it and the town, I probably exaggerated its size. But it was large enough to accommodate a huge black stove, the source of wonderful smells; a double-wide oak-sided ice-box; and an even huger kitchen table, not made of oak but of some more impressionable wood. Around the table, my parents, my aunt, my grandmother, and I could easily have fit and still have room for Bessie Messner from across the street and Dan Drivelbiss from down the hill.

If you studied the room and you listened to the women talk about the past, you learned that much of their work took place in front of the huge black stove and around the great central table. Important tools for the cooks, seasoned black frying pans, hung from a wheel attached to the ceiling; and under the edge of the table there was a sturdy stool, made by my great-grandfather Gerhart so even the shortest woman, Anna Hinterleiter, his wife and my great-grandmother, could reach the best pan for frying chicken or potatoes.

On the corner closest to the stove, the table's surface bore the brand of a meat grinder attached there when it was time to make sausage; and at its opposite corner, closer to the sink than the stove, the table would always wear the mark of a hot iron left there too long when an interruption no one ever talked about had drawn the woman at work away from her post. You could wonder about what had caused the desertion of her sacred duty, but *that was just imagination*, you'd be told, if you tried to voice your theory.

When I was not quite five years old, my theories were limited. Reading back from after Wiconisco, of this I am sure: no one ever got caught in a corner in that kitchen, neither for a private chat or to endure lectures on manners. The kitchen was large; it smelled good; and, in winter, it was the warmest place in the house, and the ample space that allowed women to do their work without knocking one another over like a row of dominoes also provided escape routes. A kid who grew bored with the "he said," "she said," and "you don't say" of adult gossip and who could get one adult to say "Yes, Bill, you're excused," could scamper away into a more interesting area, my grandfather's pharmacy, reduced by his death to a soda fountain and sundries store.

Reduced? Soda fountains have ice cream; magazines are full of alluring pictures. The treasures were just one doorway away from the kitchen. Fleeing in that direction would allow a kid (that would be me) to escape, unless an adult yodeled after him, "Bill Boy, Bill Boy, come back and put a sweater on if you're goin' in there." Bill Boy would listen because, if he didn't, the next time the adult gossip grew boring, getting excused from the table would be more difficult. Obedience was easy enough in winter: there was always a sweater at hand.

Then we moved to Harrisburg. The kitchen in our new house was another story. There was no room in it for an icebox, even though the refrigerator that arrived from Monkey Wards on the same day we got there from Wiconisco was half the width of the oak-sided wonder. The icebox got to live on the back porch where, in winter, the world turned damned cold. I wondered why we had to put ice in it at all and why I still had to empty the drip pan. One of the physics whizzes at Edison eventually explained the mystery to me. You can Google it if you need to.

The table we squeezed into the smaller space of Harrisburg's kitchen was a piker compared to the center of all things we'd had in Wiconisco. When there were just four of us—my mother, father, grandmother, and me—we fit around it, but the one backed up against the silverware drawer (that was me) had better make sure that utensils for four were already on the table before he sat down: otherwise, he'd be subjected to raised eyebrows from three directions. Nothing would be said, but, believe me, raised eyebrows can scream.

Before a year was up, my sister Barbara Jane came on board. At first that didn't change things because my mother, the meals-on-wheels lady, fed her elsewhere; but when Barbie was big enough to sit in a high chair, the space shrank. Good thing she was a quiet baby and not a food-thrower. And then, when it came time for Aunt Marion to visit for the better part of a summer, we'd move to the dining room, just enough bigger than the kitchen that we all could sit, even if we didn't quite fit. Then, at the end of August, Aunt Marion would go back to Havertown to teach Home Ec to the mainliners; the rest of us would squeeze back into the kitchen.

As in Wiconisco, the Harrisburg kitchen was full of talk, but my father didn't like to interrupt his eating with anything more than "pass the potatoes," and I was learning from him to chew the food, not the fat. When Aunt Marion was there, our voices weren't missed because she and my grandmother carried on the Wiconisco tradition of "Give us this day our daily gossip." My mother would mostly listen and occasionally look amused. When the serving plates were empty, she would turn on the hot water, gather up dishes, and begin to wash. If I hadn't moved fast, gotten an excused-from-the-table card, and followed my father into other regions, I'd be stuck where I was for how long the deity alone might know, rammed up against the silverware drawer behind me and squashed against the table in front. There was no exit aside from crawling under the table, if that could be managed in slow-low-movement-stuffed-stomach mode, because my mother would be standing in the only thru lane, washing the dishes. Then the catechism would begin. And it would last as long as a Quaker meeting.

The topics? Most of the time the focus was on all my relatives, my father's side, the Gerharts and the Keens, and my mother's side, the Billheimers, one Tempe Jane Davenport, one Byron Crampton, the Billheimers, and the Parkers, particularly the Parkers. Though my mother had learned a lot about the Gerharts and the Keens during her years in Wiconisco, she was the lore maven regarding the troops from Indiana, and most particularly the Quakers who had come there from North Carolina. I was used to family history from walks with my mother. The rhythm of walking stimulated her memory and her loquacity.

Sometimes, however, when my behavior hadn't been up to snuff, she would jump the fence into the Pasture of Good Breeding lit up by the efficacy of the Inward Light. These lessons would cause me to squirm, but I did listen. And, as it turned out, some of them still invade my thoughts. The lessons were a bit like a marriage—for better or for worse. None of these moral exercises was more lasting than the one I was given when I brought home from school the comment of a classmate that employed the n-word, uttering, for some reason I couldn't explain, "Some nigger kids came to our school today."

My mother dropped a dish on the floor: "Bill, you will not use that word!" It was the loudest statement she'd ever made in my direction. "Where did you hear that?"

Choosing my words very carefully, I explained that at recess, just after a mother and two children had arrived at the room of the head teacher, Miss Huber, some of the guys were saying those children wouldn't be coming to Forney because we didn't have those children at Forney. They'd probably be sent to Vernon. "And, Mama, they weren't saying 'those children'; they were using the word I mustn't use."

"Yes, Bill, you are never to use that word. The mother and children who came to your school are colored people and that is how you refer to them."

"I'm sorry, Mama, I didn't know."

"Well, Bill, now you do. You sit there while I tell you about the Parkers."

I knew I was in for a long one this time.

My mother told me about the Parkers, Quakers who came from England to Nantucket and worked in the whaling industry and eventually made their way to coastal North Carolina and again worked in the whaling industry. Then they moved west to an area on Polecat Creek near Greensboro, North Carolina, where they joined a Quaker meeting. This all happened before the Civil War. My Parker ancestors, she said, were abolitionists, unlike the Parkers in Virginia who grew cotton and owned slaves. When slaves were being sold, the North Carolina Quakers would pool their resources and outbid the slave owners. Some of the people they bought didn't have last names. They became Parkers, or Hoskins, or Binfords. The slave owners who had been outbid hated the Quakers, threatened them, and did everything they could to get back the colored people who had been bought by the Quakers. So the Quakers sent those threatened to Indiana and Illinois where they would be able to live as free people. That was their hope, in any case. We know, she said, that wasn't always true.

Eventually, my ancestors left North Carolina and also went to Indiana—to Richmond, where there were many Quakers. "Segregation," my mother said as she neared the ending of her sermon. "You've witnessed segregation, Bill. Segregation is wrong. People are segregated by being kept from living wherever they can afford to. There are colored people in Harrisburg who can afford to live in the Forney area, but they're kept from buying houses there."

That wasn't quite true, I later discovered. There was a lawyer named Carter who lived at 1831 Market Street. I remember because I delivered the *Patriot* to his house. I met him at least once, though usually it was his manservant who paid me and, at Christmastime, gave me a whole dollar, an outstanding tip in those days, the kind that fosters memory. Mr. Carter certainly could afford to live in the Forney area, and he had influential friends—Dr. Charles Crampton, for one, a connection to the most powerful white politician of Harrisburg, M. Harvey Taylor. Since Mr. Carter didn't have any children to enroll in Forney School, he wasn't going to upset the status quo. Believe me, this is a shortened version of that evening's catechism. By the time she'd finished, my mother had washed each dish at least three times, and it was too late for me to do my math homework. I went to bed, but I didn't sleep very well.

It was my first lesson in segregation. I'd heard the word before, but I hadn't understood it. I then began to realize it was real, that it existed in Harrisburg, that Forney was a seg-regated school, that the central YMCA was a segregated gym and pool, and that the golf clubs where I caddied on Sundays were segregated courses. My mother had been as angry as I had ever seen her when she told me about segregation. I didn't yet know that as a child in Richmond she'd lived on the wrong side of the tracks. There's more than one form of segregation.

One activity available to grade-school boys in Harrisburg wasn't segregated. It was the Gra-Y, a program of athletic events that ran throughout the school year. The Gra-Y, at least the part of it on the hill, the Edison area, was run by our neighbor, Frank Roth, who would be my Latin teacher when I got to John Harris. All the good players in fifth and sixth grade at Forney played against our counterparts at all of the grade schools that fed into Edison and then John Harris.

Most of these grade schools weren't segregated. Allison School was nearly segregated because it was almost entirely a school of black children. Actually, there were a few white children at Allison—my cousin Jeanne Gerhart, for one. She lived at 1201 Market Street, which put her in the Allison district. My mother explained that where you lived was used to segregate people. She believed that people who could afford it should be able to live wherever they wished at no extra cost. My Uncle Bill and Aunt Ruth, Jeanne's parents, chose to live at 1201 Market, my mother told me. She didn't explain why, but I took her word for it. I'd been handed a lesson at segregated Forney school, and my mother made darn sure I did my homework so I wouldn't forget it. I now know there was a lot more I needed to learn. Yeah, there still is.

In my final year at Forney, there was a Gra-Y track meet at John Harris. I participated and placed second in the broad jump, not yet renamed, and anchored a relay team that also placed second. But the real stars of the track meet were the boys from Allison. I remember particularly Alton Gaines, who won the high jump. The Allison boys also won the relay and a lot of other races. I was impressed.

It was time to go to Edison. At first, it looked like segregation all over again: all the students in 7-4, the section I was assigned to, were white. But the gym classes weren't segregated. I had gym with Alton Gaines. In two-hand touch football, Miles Gibbons led us to a victory over Alton Gaines's section, but, believe me, it was hard to get two hands on Alton when he had the ball. In basketball, Eugene Britten and Alton were the stars of the section that beat ours, though we'd been favored to win. Again, I was impressed. These guys were good.

Near the end of seventh grade, in assembly one day, the principal, Mr. Miller, explained the four educational tracks available to us the following year. We could elect to enter vocational training, secretarial training, general training, or academic training. When I told my parents as Mr. Miller had instructed us to do, they said I would be entering the academic track. That was fine with me, because I was eager to study Latin. At the beginning of eighth grade, I discovered that Willie Jones and Stanley Braxton were also eager to study Latin. Segregation of my education had finally ended. It was about time.

Six years later, I entered Dickinson College. Segregation all over again.

CHAPTER SIX

An Inventory of Adolescence: The Games We Played in the Park

Reservoir Park has two reservoirs. Back in the day, the lower one was called the *open reservoir*. It was open in the sense that it didn't have a lid on it. (Was it September 11th that changed that?) From the point of view of a kid on a hot summer day, it wasn't open at all but fenced to keep him and the public from using it as a swimming pool. It was (is) located lower down, not far from the Eighteenth and Walnut entrance to the park, just up a bit behind the tennis courts at about where Nineteenth Street would cut across the park if it were allowed to do so. We played softball near it, contending with trees for any distance in our hits; once in a while someone would drive a ball into the reservoir. Littler kids threw stones over the fence and listened for the *plunk*. In a course on the city, the open reservoir of my memory probably would have been called a major asset; but since you couldn't legally swim in it, I surely undervalued it. Moreover, the water that came out of it was so heavily laced with chlorine that my father would drive to a spring outside of town to fill up jugs rather than drink the city water.

The other reservoir was (is) up at the high point of the park. It was (is) called the *covered reservoir* because it *was* (*is*) covered; and its cover *was* a major asset, being a huge flat grassy expanse, maybe the largest flat expanse in Harrisburg not controlled by a school district or the Harrisburg Senators Baseball Club. It was a boon to families and kids old enough to be on their own during the long hot summer days when they shared the space with old men walking dogs and the regular Susquehanna River Valley scourge known as a cloud of gnats. On humid summer afternoons, these pests were so numerous that their presence during a ball game did more than the sun to blind fielders, causing them to lose track of fly balls. Yes, Adam, even an Edenic greensward has its warts and moles!

We played all sorts of games on the reservoir's grass cover, taking care not to run into the squat round metal turrets (for ventilation, I think) that interrupted the space here and there. I myself took part in baseball games, both hard- and softball varieties; football games, tackle and touch; races on foot and bike; kite-flying; *Baby in the Hat*; and general hell-raising, an activity that, in later adolescence, was punctuated by intermittent quaffing from ice-cold quart bottles in brown paper bags.

In a macadam-covered area adjacent to the grass field, I tried to learn to square dance under the instruction of older folks who belonged to some kind of preservation-of-archaic-activities society that met in the Y during the winter months; in the summer, they arrived up in the park dressed like the chorus from *Oklahoma* and ready to dance. They appeared to welcome new blood and would exercise any of us they could corral. We were reluctant at first, but, being talked into giving it a shot by some lively older ladies, we found the workout was worthwhile because, true to the types they were imitating, they had come prepared to feed us with fried chicken, ham and cheese sandwiches, vinegar slaw, Utz potato chips, and big cuts of pie from the picnic baskets they'd toted along. And Cloverdale soft drinks to wash that great grub down.

Dancing does have its rewards—one delight leading to others. Loosened up by those experienced square-dancing ladies, Joe Fiedler, Bill Greenawalt, and I began to visit teen dances at the YWCA, where girls our own age tried to coax us away from the ping-pong table and onto the dance floor. Then it was on to the high school dances, where we tried to coax cheerleaders and majorettes to drive with us up to the lookout and join in the parking games that took place just off the road that edged the grass field of the covered reservoir. Joe Fiedler called these events the Crinoline Olympics.

The high point of Harrisburg was such a useful place that I gave it a gold star on my blessings list. I'm really glad it was wide open and almost uncluttered when I was a kid. Unfortunately, a recent mayor's enthusiasm for museums has resulted in a huge building that gobbles up quite a lot of what used to be open space. Joe Fiedler says he's been a good mayor, but even good men make mistakes. Someone else said that nowadays kids don't give a shit for open space for playing the archetypal American games unless they're on an organized team with coaches and uniforms. Too true, too true!

Other than the Crinoline Olympics, a nighttime event, most of the game-playing took place during the day, particularly on weekends, when older guys with jobs gathered for softball—or on long June and July evenings that allowed time for a game between supper and the fall of darkness. Wayne English, my next-door neighbor and a member of John Harris's baseball team, was one of the players. Because my mother thought he was a nice young man, I was allowed to tag along with Wayne. Sometimes I'd be chosen and stuck in right field. Well, you've got to start somewhere.

Then, one Monday night in the fall, after daylight saving time had ended, a new scoutmaster of our troop at Fourth Reformed Church surprised us by dispensing with the meeting's usual rigmarole and, without explaining why, told each of us to grab a ground cloth from the supply closet.

"Are we going to sleep out? It's Monday; we have school tomorrow. Don't we need tents?" blurted a chorus of young worriers (yeah, even at the tenderfoot stage there are worriers).

"No, you don't need tents. Just grab ground cloths and hop in the back of the bottled gas truck outside." We knew the truck; it was our usual conveyance to jamborees and when we collected old newspapers for the church or canned goods for the needy. We did as we were told. As the truck bumped its way along the potholed streets, we realized we were on a familiar route: up through the park, past the open reservoir, Devil's Dip, and the Elk, to the covered reservoir.

At the top, Mr. Kramer instructed us to bring the ground cloths and follow him. "You, too, Wolfie," he shouted at a kid who was already complaining about camping out without a sleeping bag, a tent, or the patrol cooking kit. Wolfie was always hungry, and I would have bet he had candy bars stuffed in his jacket pockets. We followed Mr. Kramer out into the center of the vast field.

"OK, boys, spread out your ground cloths and lie down," he said, doing the same himself. We followed his lead.

"Now look at the stars," he said. We looked. I'd never seen so many stars. Once in a while, I'd seen starlight that made its way down through the obscuring hills, the heavy roof of maple leaves that covered the streets, and the city lights; but here there were millions of stars.

"Alright, boys," Mr. Kramer said, "who can tell me where the big dipper is?" Peterson, a kid who had recently moved from Nebraska and had seen the fully illuminated night sky before, responded with the alacrity of a shavetail cadet: "It's right over there, aiming toward the North Star."

"The *what* star?" Wolfie growled.

Peterson was a know-it-all, so when he repeated his answer, "The North Star," he did it with the sneering tonality that implies the unspoken insult *as even a dumbass like you should know.*

I was glad Wolfie had asked the question that had been on the tip of my tongue, and doubly glad when Mr. Kramer chimed in with a hearty "Righto, my boy!" Mr. Kramer was eager to turn out an Eagle Scout from the ragged lot of prospects he'd found at the Fourth Reformed Church. Snot-noses at the premier troop in Harrisburg referred to our band as the Fourth Reformed School Troop. Well, Mr. Kramer had found his candidate, I thought, feeling a great relief because, before Peterson had joined up and immediately begun to raise the tone, Mr. Kramer had been focusing on me. I was one of the few kids who had made it to First Class, but I knew Star Scout was about as far as I wanted to go.

Maybe Mr. Kramer sensed building resentment among our numbers, because he managed to take our minds away from festering plans of revenge against the know-it-all by pointing out other constellations, telling us, in the process, what a constellation was, and asking no more questions that only Peterson would try to answer. There are some definite drawbacks to the Socratic method!

When we finally rolled up our ground cloths and headed back to the gas company truck, my head was full of names and myths and starlight. Later that week, I walked downtown to the library and checked out a book all about the stars. For a moment, I contemplated giving Peterson a run for his money. But that reaction didn't last long. Then Peterson found out about the premier troop and left the Fourth Reformed School gang to join up with the superior types. Soon afterward, I was once again a candidate for Eagle-Scouthood in Mr. Kramer's eyes. I left, too.

Other games went on elsewhere in the park, making it to me a huge forested Olympic stadium. Down toward Twentieth and Walnut and near the picnic pavilions was a well-equipped playground. It had baby swings and big-kid swings, a jungle gym and chinning bars, a really high sliding board, and an elemental merry-go-round which two or three adolescent boys could muscle up to a speed that would give little kids a hair-raising ride.

Nearby there was a croquet court where old farts gathered to hammer the crap out of one another's colored sphere and hawk lungers on the grass. Once I saw one old guy fail to direct his spit over the edge and dribble it on the playing surface. From the reaction of his opponents, you would have thought he'd defiled the carpet in the Oval Office. They were armed, and if they'd moved a bit faster, the feckless spitter might have found his head rolling out of the park and down Walnut Street.

In an area east of the croquet courts, an archery range was set up. I sometimes saw girls a year or so younger than I shooting arrows at targets backed up with bales of hay. Joe Fiedler said one of these junior Dianas was the sister of the head majorette at John Harris and that folks in the know thought she had a good chance of competing internationally. I don't know whether she did. I was disinclined to get really close to any female armed with a bow and arrow and recognized for her accuracy. What if the irritability of the old croquet players spread to other contestants in the paradise?

It was in another part of the park that I spent most of my spare time. For as long as I could remember, less than a block up from the entrance at Eighteenth and Walnut, there were tennis courts. Also as long as I could remember, the courts were seldom used for tennis, except by Larry Fink and a kid who went away to school each September but came back in the summer to stay with a relative on Whitehall Street.

In the winter, the firemen would flood one of the courts when it got cold enough for water to freeze, and lots of kids and a few adults would congregate, intending to skate but mostly falling on their butts. Red Schaeffer and the other guys who played hockey, who could actually skate, preferred the ponds out in Bellevue Park. Little kids stayed away from the ponds because the ice could give way and someone might drown. I didn't much care to slide around on the ice at either place, but occasionally I hung out with Joe Fiedler and Bill

Greenawalt at the frozen court. We hoped to meet interesting girls and maybe even get to massage their bruises.

I think it was in 1950 or '51 that the folks who ran the park decided to put one of the neglected tennis courts to use as a basketball court by installing metal backboards on iron poles and painting keys and foul lines at either end. What geniuses! Before long, that court was heavily used, so much on weekends that we had to dole out playing time for the arriving hordes by organizing team tournaments. Sometimes five guys would arrive early and claim the court for "ducks" or other hotdogging activities until another five would arrive to challenge them. While the first game was being played, other fives would arrive and wait their turns to take on the winners. If you had a good five, you could play until hunger, thirst, or the lack of light drove you from the place.

On a winter weekend when it snowed, Tommy Gray, who lived close by on Whitehall, would get out early and shovel the snow off the court. When the sun obliged, the surface would be cleared and dry before noon, and the games would begin. During high school days and, later, when guys were home on vacation from college, most of the good players in Harrisburg spent some time on that court: Dave Graybill, Dick Davies, Bob Nelson, and Rusty Owens from my generation at John Harris; Sonny Crist from uptown; and Tommy Gray, who, for a couple of years, started for Catholic High.

Then some of the guys got cars and we'd round up our five, dubbed the Reservoir Vagabonds by Joe, and take the game on the road to Melrose or Riverside, or downstream to Steelton or across the Susquehanna to Camp Hill.

In these games, there were no substitutes. Five guys (and a ball) was the limit for one of those old cars, particularly when it was sweltering and we rode back to Reservoir Park without the benefit of showers in sweating camaraderie. Sometimes we'd make a stop near a neighborhood bar whose proprietor didn't check IDs, and the oldest-looking among us, often Bill Greenawalt, would nip in to purchase quarts of Stegmaier's or Yuengling's. What satisfaction there was in quaffing our illegal beer! "Oh, Bill, that's not a blessing," my mother would have said.

Competitive sports weren't the only activities that made Reservoir Park a blessing. We had culture, too! And of that my mother heartily approved. The center of cultural life was the band shell. It sat (it still sits) at the bottom of the slope that ran down from the park's high point toward Walnut Street. It had rows and rows of benches for civilized spectators and, higher up the slope, a large grassy area where nature lovers, usually families with rutschy kids full of piss and vinegar, could spread out blankets.

During the summer, there were band concerts on Thursday evenings and miscellaneous events on Sundays. Since I was learning to blast the trombone for Frank Iorio in the Edison Junior High band, I'd go to listen to the Moose and American Legion bands. My mother approved. I heard some pretty good cornet solos by Mr. Rheim, who, as a young man, had played with the Marine Band, and one hell of a lot of marches. For these, I'd sit and listen or lie on the grass (sans blanket) on the higher hillside. Finally, at the end of ninth grade, I got to play my trombone in the band shell at my class's commencement from Edison Junior High and to enjoy listening to the trombone solo (you know, the one that goes "Tramp! tramp! tramp! the Boys are marching)" by a real trombone player, my friend and classmate Jerry Lego. My mother said that the event was one of her blessings, so I mentally added it to my list.

On Sunday evenings, I didn't pay much attention to the improving fare being offered, unless one of the dance studios was hosting a review and the stage was filled with long-legged girls in tutus. When there was nothing more interesting to watch, or when you were thirsty or hungry from the rigors of summertime activities at the playground or at a concert, you could head to a nearby refreshment stand and buy a Coke or a Crass's orange soda or root beer or a Hershey's ice cream slice in a wide-mouthed cone. You'd transact your business with Horstick or Shammo, the guys who ran the place. During the day, it was usually Horstick on duty, maybe because Shammo was busy at the big-deal grocery store that bore his last name down at Seventeenth and Walnut.

Horstick was an extremely tall guy and not undergrown in any way. He always looked a little bit bent over from trying not to bump his head on the shack's low ceiling. On the evenings of band shell concerts and other events, Horstick would be joined by Shammo. Shammo was shorter than Horstick, so there was no chance he'd clunk his head on the ceiling, but he was about as wide as he was high. It was only by an elaborate sidestep-and-squeeze act that they could get by one another to wait on customers. Sometimes they had another helper who was nearly as wide as Shammo and only a couple of inches shorter than Horstick.

The shack wasn't air-conditioned, and even in the evenings when there was a breeze, it was amazing to watch the three of them sweat. Horstick would develop some major rings on his shirt beneath his armpits, and Shammo and the other guy looked as if they'd just emerged from a swim in the open reservoir with their clothes on. It was a good thing they didn't cook soup in there. When they debouched from the shack at the end of a hot and busy summer evening, they reminded me of the endless profusion of clowns that exploded from one small Crosley at the Shriners' circus. Too bad the elephants weren't nearby to give them a shower.

Of these three guys, I got to know Horstick best, because I would sometimes visit the shack during the day to buy bubblegum packets, which included baseball cards. Once Horstick knew my interest, he'd tell me when earlier customers had found some new faces in a recently arrived box of cards. He'd also save soda bottle crowns, which I'd begun to collect. Years later, I impressed collectors at a Crownvention in New Cumberland with the large number of bottle caps from Crass's orange soda and root beer I offered for trading.

Collections cost money, so when the band shell fare didn't excite me, I'd supplement my paper route earnings by heading for the band shell and collecting the soda bottles people weren't going to bother returning for the deposit. They'd leave them lying on the grass where the empties would send out signals of light reflected from the overhead lamps. In an evening, I could usually collect twenty-five or thirty bottles, enough to cover the cost of as many baseball cards or get me into a double feature at the Penway, the Grand, or the Roxy and several Wednesday afternoon "buddy shows" at the Capitol. (What a deal—a double feature, a Spy Smasher serial episode, and all the bugs you could carry home!)

Labor Day would come, and there'd be the summer-ending festival of Kipona Day down in River Front Park, with swimming events and boat races, and at Island Park the Senators would usually play a double header. Once, a boxing ring was set up and local fighters had at one another for part of the afternoon. But not much happened in Reservoir Park. Horstick swept out the soda shack and battened down the shutters for one last time. I helped him one year and got to keep all the bottle caps I found lurking in the corners and under the ice cream freezer. Then, in a day or two, we'd go back to school at Edison or John Harris. It would still be too hot to enjoy being inside all day long, but in a couple of weeks it'd grow cooler, and the smell of leaves on the sidewalk would holler "football!"

On Friday nights I'd hustle to collect the weekly charge from as many of my newspaper customers as I could get to before suppertime. Back home, I'd bolt down my meal and head out as briskly as possible for the Friday-night game at Catholic High, the fast getaway calculated to limit my mother's questions before the screen door slammed and enable me to claim later that I hadn't heard her ask. I thought my father knew where I was headed and hoped he'd allay her fear that I was running off to join the circus. I heard the circus bit voiced so often by my mother, my grandmother, and my Aunt Marion that I began to think someone in our family had actually skipped town with Ringling Brothers. Later on, after reading Mark Twain and a few other authors who promoted the American theme of wanderlust, I concluded that, for most Americans and probably for my relatives, it was simply an enduring American cliché.

When I reached the corner of Twenty-First and Whitehall, there'd be a throng of Catholic High students walking up Market Street to the school and then around back to the proper entrance. They had ID cards and could get in cheap. A sprinkling of adults would go that way too, but I'd forego it, detouring up Taylor Boulevard and taking a path up from the edge of the road through the tangle of wild growth on the hillside below the football field. I'd join other kids and even some older guys at the far end of the field, where, word had it, someone with wire cutters had been at work. I'd linger in the bushes until the coast was clear, then join the crowd of urchins who'd slipped through the cut fence and high-tailed it up the chalk hill on the north side of the field to watch the game.

If one of the gang had brought along a ball, we'd spend halftime in a football free-for-all in a large open area behind the goalposts at the far end of the field. For kids our age, football was a kind of contagious disease: you'd watch maybe half of the organized contest; then, when the teams headed back to the locker room, you were hungry for some action of your own. Someone hurled the ball in the air, a brave soul caught it, and everyone else tried to tackle him. Often these contests would continue throughout the second half of the game, finally being brought to an end by the cleanup crew shooing us off on the coattails of the last stragglers in the departing crowd. What was the hurry? We could sleep late on Saturday morning. And in the afternoon, John Harris, lacking lights, would play its game. We'd have to sit in the stands.

At John Harris, there was no chalk hill, nor any unused area for a football free-for-all. But if John Harris won (they usually did), the high school band would march from the field to Market Street and then up and down a hill to Seventeenth and Market, the tooters, drummers, and blasters playing all the marches in their repertoire, the majorettes twirling and high-stepping at the head of the band, and the cheerleaders running along beside the noise encouraging the accompanying crowd to sing, cheer, and shout the praises of our victorious boys. Oh, to be one of them!

In this way, the fall would turn, weekend after weekend, until the end of the local football season on Thanksgiving Day. Then the team and the band would be bused down to Hershey to the annual season-ender against archrival William Penn. The younger guys and the Harris boys who weren't on the team or in the band would bum rides to Hershey with Russ Mills or some other older guy with a car to watch the game and the elaborate halftime show put on by both teams' bands accompanied by majorettes and flag-twirlers and culminating in the John Harris trombone choir playing the traditional Thanksgiving hymn, "We Gather Together to Ask the Lord's Blessing."

Oh, how I wanted to stop being a mere spectator and wear a John Harris uniform. Being unaffiliated had its advantages, primarily that few extracurricular learning programs were shoved my way by overearnest adults. I was capable of choosing what I wanted to do without the aid of parents or scoutmasters or a manners-conscious aunt. I could always read books, the best way I'd found to be left alone; and I had found jobs that paid, the best way I'd found *not* to have to listen to the constant worrying about money at 2033.

But I didn't want to be alone all the time, and I thought I could moderate the solitary and the social by going out for football. In a seventh-grade phys ed class at Edison, I had managed to punt a football further than anyone else. Coach Atticks suggested I come out for football and gave me a permission slip to take home for a parent's signature. When I asked my parents to sign, they exclaimed almost in unison that I was too little and cited my Uncle Donald's loss of teeth at Quakerly Earlham as the reason no son of theirs would play the dangerous game.

I *wasn't* too little. I was taller than most of the guys in my class. Yeah, I know, I hadn't put on enough flesh to cover my bones so that I didn't look like a scarecrow, and my parents were quick to point that out. So what? Most of the other guys my age were as skinny as I was, except for Willie Wallbanger, who ate Tastykakes and pies between meals and stuffed broken beer pretzels in his pockets to sneak snacks during afternoon algebra class. My mother knew Willie—how could she miss that bulk lumbering up the street? She was quick to point out that if Willie tackled me and fell on top, I'd be a sack of broken bones and maybe suffocated. But, hell, he'd never catch me. He was too fat to walk, let alone run.

When I told Mr. Atticks how my parents had reacted, he said, "Too bad, Bill, but if you don't have a parent's signature, you can't play." Dreams of a letter on my sweater and a shapely cheerleader or majorette on my arm melted away faster than butter in the hot sun.

Lacking a uniform, a coach, and any likelihood of a date, even to a run-of-the-mill flick at the lowly Penway, I tried to satisfy myself with tag football games in alleys and on playgrounds. Then, the year I entered the tenth grade at John Harris, the guys from Reservoir Park formed a sandlot team. Foregoing any conversation with my parents, I joined the Reservoir Vagabonds. All in all, we were a ragtag bunch. I had a helmet, shoulder pads, and a boxer's mouthpiece, and I was better equipped than some of the guys. The Vagabonds didn't practice, but each fall for three years we played five or six games against teams from Bellevue Park, Herr Street near the Armory, Derry Street, and Shipoke. Everyone played both ways. I was either a fullback or an end on offense and an end or a linebacker on defense. I got to do a hell of a lot of blocking and tackling. I didn't lose any teeth, but when my left knee hurts now that I'm in my eighties, I remember the linebacker from Shipoke who stopped me from scoring on the one-yard line.

Throughout the fall, on afternoons and on Sundays all day long, those of us who weren't wearing John Harris uniforms were back where we'd spent most of the summer, at the basketball court rescued from a life of tennis. And even in good weather during the winter, that's where most of us would hang out, playing ducks or waiting our turns to take on the winners. Why not? It was comfortable territory, close to soda fountains, pinball machines, and the Penway Theater. And at the lower or Eighteenth Street entrance to the park there was a grassy area backed up by two colossal pillars salvaged from an important building downtown.

In the early evening, exhausted by the day's games, guys would lounge on the grass like so many denim-clad Romans and eye passing cars, hoping for one filled with cheerleaders and majorettes—usually with no results. All the while we'd natter on about what a drag this place was until someone, most likely Paulie Krebs, would ask, "What's at the Penway?" And someone, damn near always Joe Fiedler, would answer, "You already seen it; you went last night and they ain't changed the shows yet." That might not keep Paulie and others who'd already seen it from going again. None of our families had TVs.

From time to time, the thirstier sorts would drag themselves across the street to Bert's for a fountain Coke and a check on the latest comic books and other magazines. You could find practically every comic book there: Superman and his many imitators, *Disney Comics* and *Looney Tunes,* and even the high-toned *Classic Comics* some guys cribbed book reports from. *Life* and *Look* and *Saturday Evening Post* were there, and the *Police Gazette,* the *Farmer's Almanac,* and the *Grit,* and a high shelf full of racier mags with pictures of scantily clad girls on the covers. You could also scope out newspapers from Harrisburg and Philadelphia, but I don't remember ever seeing the *New York Times* for sale in the heart of the Republican T.

A nearby alternative for slaking thirst and wasting time was the Ryder's Dairy Store, about the same distance from our grassy forum as Bert's but in the other direction. There, you could get a bottle of Coke, a popsicle, or, if you were flush, a super sundae. Also, the local lovelies were more likely to go there than to Bert's because Ryder's had booths equipped with selectomatics listing all the popular hits loaded on Ryder's jukebox. And best of all, Ryder's had not one, but two of those greatest of all possible lures for a kid with a nickel in his pocket: pinball machines!

When I first started to play pinball machines, they were pretty basic—five balls for a nickel, eight or ten lights to hit, a strait or two to squeeze through, and some potholes where you could lose your ball halfway down. To roll the ball where you wanted it to go, you had to bang the machine; to roll it back toward the top, you had to lift up the lower end. Either of these maneuvers was likely to *tilt* the damn thing and end your turn. Then, for an adolescent addict, one of the greatest events of modernity occurred. The benefactors of humanity who manufactured pinball machines installed flippers. With flippers, a player could redirect the ball from the bottom back up to the top and keep his turn alive almost forever. All of the machines that ever did duty in Ryder's had flippers. Did I say they did duty? Yeah, they were like sentinels standing at attention at the door to a wonderful world!

One summer when I had a real job and was supposed to be saving money for college, I invested the better part of a semester's tuition in the pinball machines while I listened to endless repetitions of "Cold, Cold Heart," "Wheel of Fortune," and "It's a Sin," paid for by the local ladies or any guys they could induce to feed the jukebox as part of the pre-courting ritual.

During all the time I wasted in these two adjuncts to the park, the event that stands out most prominently in memory occurred on a hot Saturday afternoon in August the year before I would be packed off to college by my aspiring parents. Often, near the end of summertime, relatives of my friends would come to visit, sometimes for the educational purpose of visiting the state capitol and checking out the murals or, more likely, to spend time at Hershey Park in the huge swimming pool (long since gone) or to knock one another about in the bumper cars or to scream their lungs out on the hair-raising rollercoaster in the amusement park.

Jack Livingood had a cousin who hailed from Somerset, where the Livingood clan had lived before moving to Harrisburg. That summer, she came to visit, and though Jack himself was too busy working on his '34 Plymouth to bring her up to the park and introduce her, Jack's sister Patty did the job. This cousin—I'll call her Debbie because she was every bit as shapely as Debbie Reynolds—arrived with Patty; and the two of them sat on the bench along the side of the basketball court. Patty was identifying the sweaty males involved in the game. She'd point to one, then another of us, and Debbie would nod and smile as she checked off each identification. After a while, we realized that Patty was explicating the heart-surrounded initials some of the would-be lotharios had carved into the bench. And it certainly looked as if Debbie was taking it all in.

We were playing a game of twenty-one—one point per bucket, no foul shots (the three-pointer hadn't been invented yet), and you had to win by at least two.

The presence of Debbie spurred a lot of hotdogging and missed shots, so it took forever to finish the game. When the game was over, all the guys who'd been showing off were thirsty; it was time to hit Ryder's. Joe Fiedler, our local Sir Walter Raleigh, invited the girls to come along. I was surprised they accepted, because, as anyone could see, our overheated group was sweating profusely.

At the store, the ten wet guys and the two dry girls filled up the two booths. Joe Fiedler had managed to separate Debbie from her cousin and get her into one side of the second booth, flanked by Joe on the inside and me on the outside and with three other guys facing us. I was of two minds about this arrangement: I yearned to be close to that shapely body, but I was afraid I might drown her. One of the guys in the other booth was jamming nickels in the jukebox, most likely at the instigation of Patty, who was learning fast from her visiting cousin.

Joe Fiedler had taken over as the MC of our cramped stage, handling introductions all around. With an attempt at smoothness he'd picked up from some movie he'd seen at the Penway, he announced, "This is Hunk, Paulie, and Arch," as he pointed to the guys on the other side, united by the smitten gaze they cast upon Debbie. "That shy one on your left is Bill, aka *Ish*—and I'm yours truly, young swain-about-town, Joseph J. Fiedler."

Young swain! What a ham, I thought *and why'd he refer to me by that stupid nickname he gave me?* Wet as I was, I felt more like a fish! Debbie, it turned out, would be a cheerleader for the football team when school started up in the fall back in Somerset; but for now and the next two days, she was here, she announced with a flirtatious grin. *Carpe diem!* Yeah, I did know what *carpe diem* meant, because by then I'd had several years of Latin from Soapy Roth. I was wondering how I might do just that at some other place, away from this mob. The Penway was out. Not even for love would I spend money to see a jerky flick about a talking mule. I couldn't afford a trip to Hershey, and I doubted that she'd fancy a trek downtown to the library. A walk in the park seemed like a better idea, but how was I going to get her away from this gang of smitten competitors?

Just then, Jack Stitley entered the store, cast a glance at the crowded booths, and headed for the pinball machines. Debbie, I noticed, watched his route with interest. Was she an addict, too?

"You play pinball?" I asked.

"Oh, yes!" she exclaimed.

I grabbed her hand and hauled her out of the booth and over to the other machine. I slipped a nickel in the slot and gestured for her to play. She manned the flippers like a pro, almost winning a game for her high score. I slipped another—my last—nickel in the slot so she could play again. Joe Fiedler sidled up, placed a quarter's worth of nickels on the glass, and said, "I'm in. Where's yours, Ish? Ante up!"

But I was broke, so I said "See ya later" and surrendered the field to my well-heeled rival, getting no reply from Debbie, who was absorbed in the game.

I did see her again. It was the following evening. I was headed to a double feature of Randolph Scott at the Penway. Debbie was walking into the park with a college guy named Ken who played football and expected to start at center for his team that fall. If I hadn't realized it before, I knew, right then, I didn't have a monopoly on the many blessings offered by Reservoir Park.

CHAPTER SEVEN

Prefrontal Shortcomings: Playing Dangerous Games

I grew up in an age when most juvenile delinquents spent as much time as possible out in the fields and streets of Harrisburg playing a number of dangerous games. Why we did this is still a matter of argument whenever a few of the survivors, now in their eighties, get together at one of the spas of geriatric palaver. Testosterone? Can't remember when I had too much of that coursing through my system. My now-fifty-year-old daughter is a big advocate of the delayed prefrontal development of adolescent males to explain their uncontrollable and potentially life-threatening behavior. Her argument contends that reckless behavior continues up to about age thirty-five and offers a collective explanation for the binges and assaults performed by members of Data Whitcha Yu and Lumpa Lamba Psi.

Back when I was putting notches on my personal belt of youthful stupidity, in addition to playing unsupervised sandlot football, I boxed in the Gra-Y and the scout troop and wrestled at the Y, where a Penn State graduate was trying to whip up enthusiasm for the sport. Frankly, the experience served me well, or at least I thought so, because sometimes fistfights would flare up and a guy would have to try to defend himself. Yeah, fists, they were the anger weapons of juvies in my day, along with an occasional tire iron, and once, to my recollection, a plumb bob wrapped in a handkerchief. I heard there were knives but never saw one in action, except in the movies; and no kid I knew ever wielded a more dangerous firearm than a BB gun in a conflict with his contemporaries. Mostly, we used fists, and mostly I was able to hold my own, usually escaping without any blood loss.

My mother's Quakerly proscription against guns included BB guns, so, unlike Ralphie of rabbit-eared pajama fame, I never had one of those dangerous weapons; but almost every other kid in the neighborhood owned one. Bill Greenawalt even had one with a telescopic sight! In the fields out beyond Union Deposit there were lots of cows. Jack and Eddie Livingood and one of the Potter boys all owned some version of a BB gun. With these weapons strapped across the handlebars, they'd ride bikes out in search of cows. When they'd find a field full of ruminating beasts, they'd check to see that no farmers were around, then get to work peppering the girls with BBs. The game was to see whose shot would produce the most full-throated mooing. Eventually they grew bored with this contest and began shooting at one another. They first agreed that all shooters would aim low, but in the heat of the fray BBs would hit higher and higher, until one caught Eddie an inch below his right eye. They had the good sense to call it a day and, as far as I know, they didn't start up again. Eddie grew up to be a cop in Harrisburg. I wonder if he terrorized kids bearing BB guns as well as the more heavily armed hoodlums that grew like topsy in the fifties and sixties.

The only real rifle I ever saw a kid use was in the hands of John Shuey; I think it belonged to his older brother. John, scorning the BB gun as a kid's toy, used the .22 to shoot rats in the dump just beyond Twentieth and Holly. Shooting rats didn't seem like a dangerous game, and John's good aim even won the approval of adults, who saw his effort as a positive civic activity. The dump was in a hollow that ran downhill to forty feet below street level. John would sit on the upper bank and pot rat after rat. Then, all pumped up by his success as a marksman, he would scamper down into the pit. Two-thirds of the way down, he could just reach the end of a steel cable that hung from the tallest tree on the lot and haul the monkey swing back up the bank toward the top. I would sit still to fill the role of spectator. John would encourage me to join in. "Want to try it, Bill?"

"No thanks, Tarzan, I'll watch."

"OK, chicken!"

That's the way it would go, day after day. Then, on a hot afternoon in midsummer, at the end of a particularly successful rat slaughter, John bolted for the monkey swing, hauled it up near the top of the bank, leapt, and soared out into space. "Whoo-wee," he cried. Then he fell. I ran down the bank to where he lay on jars and cans and some softer cardboard cartons that had cushioned his fall and maybe saved his life. His left forearm was pinned underneath his body. He was moaning. "Oh, Bill, oh, Bill, help me, help me."

I struggled to get him to his feet and up the bank. He held his left arm across his chest with his right hand. I could see the dent in his left wrist. Fortunately, we had come to the dump on our bikes. I got him to lean on the handlebars of his bike and walk as best he could as I endeavored to wheel the bike and the boy the two blocks to his house.

His brother Dick saw us on Chestnut Street, and—after a wisecrack about bedraggled gypsies—realized that John was hurt, shut his mouth, and wheeled the wounded rat warrior the rest of the way home. I went back to the dump for my own bike, but I forgot about the .22, and as far as I know, so did everyone else. My mother would have listed that as a blessing.

When the reservoir gang went to Bert's to chug down Cokes and have free reads of the latest comic books, Joe

Fieldler, Paulie Krebs, or Jack Stitely would often promote a round of Buck Buck, a dangerous game I was willing to play. On the corner in front of Bert's was stationed a telephone pole with a streetlight attached. By the time I joined the game, this light standard had been designated the home pole for Reservoir Vagabond Buck Buck contests.

As a look at Wikipedia will show, the game has been around for a long time. Why not? Adolescent testosterone isn't a new thing either. What all the versions have in common is that at least one player climbs on another player's back. The climbing player, or, in many versions of the game, multiple players, try to break down the ridden player or players. The ridden guy or guys try to throw the rider or riders off balance so that one of them touches the ground with his foot or falls clean off. One of the riders says "Buck, Buck, how many fingers are up?" If the down man or team guesses the number of fingers up, that's theoretically another way of getting out from under; but it rarely works because—particularly when engaged in competitive activities—adolescents lie.

We usually played the game with four players on each side. The players on the down side bent at the waist, and the first guy hugged the telephone pole and tucked his head as far to the side as he could.

The next guy put his arms around the first guy's waist and tucked his head to the side. The third and fourth guys did the same. The result was a line of backs more or less parallel to the ground. The other team of four would jump, one at a time, onto the backs of the down team, the final jumper hollering, "Buck, Buck, how many fingers are up?" All the while, the down team would be trying to dump one or more of the riders by shifting suddenly from side to side as much as possible while bent over and hooked together like a line of monkeys.

When Bill Cosby started to do his Fat Albert Buck Buck routine, the Reservoir Vagabonds already knew what it was all about. Well, we thought we knew what it was all about. But I, at least, had to wait sixty years to discover the lasting effects of Buck Buck. In my late seventies, my two-mile walk three or four times a week was being slowed down to a creep not only by the left knee the Shipoke linebacker had hit but also by a back getting sorer and stiffer by the week.

My daughter Rebecca carted me off to an orthopod. I told him I remembered the hit I'd taken in a sandlot football game when I was seventeen. The doc had my knee x-rayed and declared there was nothing wrong with it. Then he x-rayed my back. "My word, Mr. Keen, what did you do to your back?"

"What's wrong with my back, Doc?"

"It looks like someone pounded on it with a baseball bat. You've got a legion of bone spurs."

"Buck Buck," I said. But I don't remember my back hurting me then. Besides, the winning team got cold drinks at

Bert's, paid for by the losers. I was always up for a Cloverdale Punch.

Frankie Fetrow had his own dangerous game. As a wizard with automobile motors, he souped up the engine of his '48 Mercury until it would go ninety miles an hour on back roads around Harrisburg, which was really fast but not quite fast enough to clear the bridge abutment that ended his life.

CHAPTER EIGHT

Advertisements Abounding: Sleeping Out in the Park

On the hot nights of July and August, people of all ages sought remedies to cool their brows and maybe nod off to sleep for a wink or two. My father took baths in water as cold as he could get it. Did he add ice cubes? Throughout the sweltering city, people sat on their front or back porches until midnight or later while fans fanned in the indoor rooms, moving the air a bit but failing to cool it.

"Why didn't you turn on the a. c?" my grandchildren ask when I launch into my tale of woe.

"The what?" I reply, playing it for all it's worth to pull their cords.

"The air-conditioning, Grandpa. Why didn't you turn on the air-conditioning?"

"Because in Harrisburg in the late 1940s and early 1950s most people didn't have air-conditioning," I declare. That sends one of them to check me out, thinking (hoping?) I've finally gone around the bend. And soon one of them is threatening to award me four Pinocchios for my geriatric fibbing. And, of course, the researchers have a case. They've gone to the Internet (didn't even have to take time to get to the library), and I'm being informed that air-conditioning dates back as far as 1915 and began its stint in movie theaters in 1925, when Willis Carrier talked Paramount into installing air-conditioning at the Rivoli Theater in New York. I know, I know: the foe of heat and humidity was around and cooling some folks even before I was born. I have the sense to shut up and avoid the suggestion that we should have gone to Kmart or Walmart and bought a unit. In a day when even from the windows of rustic shacks in Maine air conditioners have sprouted, it's a losing battle to argue that, in my youth, the people who had air conditioning in their homes were as rare as elephants in Alaska. Kmart? It didn't exist. Kresge's five-and-dime was still around, but you wouldn't find an air conditioner for sale in one of them. It wasn't until 1962 that S.S. Kresge opened the first Kmart. If Wikipedia can be trusted, the first Kmart was located in Garden City, Michigan. The store may have sold air conditioners, but that was too late to cool the brows and bods of Harrisburgers in the early 1950s.

The first boxy units I saw spouting from the windows of a house were in Bellevue Park, where wealthier people than the Keens, the Feidlers, and the Greenawalts hung out. The house that sported them belonged to the Baker family. I had gone to school with Collins Baker at Forney Grade School, but by the time the air conditioners arrived, he was attending Harrisburg Academy, a private school. As I recall, Collins's father owned one of the stores in Harrisburg that sold air conditioners when they finally got to our neck of the woods. Probably the units bulging from the windows of the Baker house were a kind of advertisement.

In those days, when the unrelenting heat and humidity of July and August bred bad tempers and dreams of snow, Bill Greenawalt and I, sometimes joined by Jack Livengood, would sleep out in Reservoir Park. We'd stake out a slightly descending slope on the hillside below Devil's Dip, put down a ground cloth, unroll our sleeping bags, and—lying on our backs—look at the stars. As the summer wore on, we saw shooting stars, and I remembered my old scoutmaster's lesson that you had to get away from the city lights to see the stars.

In the summer of 1952, Joe Fiedler, Bill Greenawalt, and I were nearing the end of our time together in Harrisburg, but none of us was acting like it yet. What I knew was that my parents expected me to go to college, and I was trying to put that out of my mind as long as possible. Bill Greenawalt was also being encouraged to apply. This was really kind of special, because Bill had been in the print shop program at John Harris and, until late in high school, hadn't considered going to college. Bill had gone to work after school and weekends for J. P. Weidenhammer Advertising Agency, making mats for advertisements, setting type, and doing pasteups for many of the well-known firms of our area—Hershey Chocolate Company, Yuengling Beer, and the York Fairgrounds among them. His boss, a guy named Frank Bratten, recognizing Bill's intelligence and industriousness, convinced him to apply to Rochester Institute of Technology. Bill did. He was accepted. And there began a great career. And there was a bonus, too, because at Rochester he met Bobbie, the beautiful young woman who would become his wife.

Late in August, the collective itch of adolescence began to get to a number of the neighborhood rowdies. Soon it would be Labor Day. The Kipona events would take place down on the Susquehanna and in River Front and Island Parks. Then it'd be back to school for the younger guys and off to work or to college for the older ones. All too soon; much too soon. And to make things worse, the weather turned hot as the hinges. Something had to give.

What gave was all restraint in damn near all the kids in the neighborhood; they came in droves to sleep out in Reservoir Park. Kids I hadn't seen in years arrived, toting makeshift bedrolls, bags of trash food, and BB guns. There were Krebses, Millers, a Daniels, a couple of Livingoods, and a number of aspiring hell-raisers I couldn't put names to. Why they needed BB guns was a mystery—maybe to defend their horde of greasy treats—maybe because they knew that Bill Greenawalt sometimes took along his BB gun, a weapon made famous by its super telescopic sight.

One of the rowdies who arrived was Wolfie, the erstwhile boy scout and reluctant stargazer. The hoard of junk food he hauled up to the park would have fed an army. It wasn't long before all hell broke loose. BB gun battles started up and spread down to Whitehall Street. Among other targets, a neighborhood cat was assaulted and made its displeasure known by unrestrained complaint. The safest place for a non-combatant was inside his bedroll, and I've already explained how hot it was. Before long, Wolfie and his cronies had shot all their BBs and eaten most of their junk food. But Wolfie wasn't anywhere close to quitting his assault upon cats and anything else that moved. During a lull in the fracas, he began to talk up a raid on a garden he knew about just outside the park on Walnut Street. He'd hit it before, he bragged, and come away with some huge tomatoes. I was surprised that Wolfie ate any veggies, but soon his troop took off on their mission.

Apparently the gardener was afflicted by the heat as well, or maybe he was just protecting what was left of his tomatoes. In any case, when the raiders arrived at his plot, he chased them away. He may even have followed them back up into the park. That was one of the theories to explain what happened shortly after Wolfie and his crew returned, winded and without an edible bite. Others favored the notion that the lady whose cat had been peppered with BBs had squealed to the authorities.

Whatever the case, the cops arrived. They came thundering down the wooded hillside shouting "It's a raid!" They rousted any guys who were actually trying to sleep out of that intention, searched the area, and discovered and confiscated the BB guns, including Bill Greenawalt's famous one with the telescopic sight. I wondered if the weapons would actually be registered at police headquarters or turn up under Christmas trees the following December.

Then they escorted us to our homes, woke up our parents, and instructed them to keep us from using Reservoir Park as our bedroom. My father grunted his assent; my mother whined, "Oh, Bill." I headed for my bedroom on the third floor, the hottest room in the house, and stewed in my own juices until I was sure my father had gone to work. Then, I skedaddled fast and spent the rest of the day away from 2033 Whitehall Street.

CHAPTER NINE

Whether I Wanted To or Not:
The Saga of the Vomiting Mailbox

The assault on the mailbox at 2033 actually began about midway through my junior year at John Harris. I'd been a better-than-average student in the academic track. I'd played along in the marching and concert bands and the orchestra. After being barred from football by my parents and cut from basketball and baseball by the coaches, I'd actually won a varsity letter in track by running and placing in the mile, the half mile, and the two-mile relay. And I'd gotten a surprisingly high score on a standardized exam sponsored by Juniata College. You'd better believe me, it was mostly verbal.

My mother smiled knowingly at the scores. My father scratched his head as if he'd discovered something out of place, a louse perhaps. Finally, he'd said, "That's good, Bill." Though he usually had trouble mustering anything in the way of praise for my academic performance (B's satisfied me but not Robert D.), I guessed he was proud of me, because when the college brochures began to arrive, he was the first to seize them. That was OK with me. I still wasn't convinced college was where I ought to be going. So I backed off and let my dad enjoy himself.

I was tired of school, tired of listening to lectures, tired of memorizing, memorizing, memorizing, tired of enduring math course after math course. I wanted to stop delivering newspapers and get a real job, making real money, maybe thirty bucks a week. I dreamed of working as a newspaper reporter or buying a fedora and a trench coat and becoming a private eye like Sam Spade. Move to Los Angeles. Hire a sarcastic but teasingly attractive secretary to spiff up my fourth-floor walk-up office. Hey, I hadn't been wasting my time. During the duller of my classes, I'd been reading pulp magazines slipped inside a textbook. Yeah, I know, impractical daydreamer. I've heard it before—from teachers, scoutmasters, my parents, even some of my super-striving classmates. But my parents still had hopes for me, and they were being encouraged by all that mail from colleges.

Soon I began to wonder whether my silence was such a good idea. Maybe I should have rained on this parade from the start. I cringed at plans to devote half the summer's weekends following junior year to visiting colleges. I only hoped those plans (pipe dreams?) went nowhere, like the canceled weekend fishing trips and baseball games of the past. My dad still had to work, work, work: but by this time, he was working for one firm and not being laid off at the end of each job. All progress comes with a cost.

While my father digested the catalogs, my mother tried to pump up my self-esteem. "Oh, Bill, you're such a good student in literature and language, and you know how to argue. You'd make a wonderful lawyer," she said.

"What makes you think I want to be a lawyer?"

"Oh, Bill," she sighed.

My father tore his attention away from Muhlenburg College, which was encouraging the recipient to join the Mules. (If Uncle Charles were still alive, he might've liked that.) Robert D. gathered in a full lung's worth of air and blew it forth: "Well, you're no damn good in math, so you're not going to be an engineer."

"What makes you think I want to be an engineer?"

It went on and on, day after day.

Actually, we did look at several colleges that summer. Given all the work both parents had done, the visits were a foregone conclusion. To kill three birds with one stone, we looked at schools in conjunction with a trip to Philadelphia to visit Aunt Marion and to see the Phillies play the Giants. Franklin and Marshall appealed to my dad. It looked OK to me, too; and our neighbor Wayne English, who'd gone there, gave the school a high rating. For a while, it was in the race. Later on, I actually looked at the college's requirements, and, finding I'd have to take more math there, I scratched it before the quarter finals. Sorry, Wayne. Sorry, Don Brauw (Don was a supersmart guy who actually went to F&M, mastered the math, and went on to become an osteopath).

One of my favorite teachers at John Harris was Mr. Roth, who'd led me through three years of Latin. He required his students to subscribe to *The Reader's Digest* because each issue included a lengthy vocabulary list. We were to figure out or look up the meanings and derivations of all the words, many of which had Latin ancestors. That was a hell of a lot more satisfying than solving math problems.

Advisors at John Harris had said Penn might be within my reach. I was surprised. Penn was an Ivy League school. I thought that meant a guy had to be very smart and/or very rich to get in. Maybe if you were a super athlete, you might make it with lower grades and less money. I didn't think I was super enough, and all the guys I knew who were, and who hoped to use their prowess to gain admission, seemed to think that at the top of the pecking order for an admissions boost was football and at the very bottom was track. Didn't Penn sponsor the relays? No dice, my buddies said, that's for sprinters and quarter-milers.

I liked the idea that Penn's location promised easy access to the Phillies and the Eagles, both teams I was rooting for back then. I probably should have kept my mouth shut, because when I didn't, and my father realized I would consider a school because it was close to professional games, he frowned a deep ditch into his forehead. I wondered if he thought I'd sell my books to pay my way to get into games. I might have. As it turned out, I removed Penn from the list because Bill Brennen said an applicant had to have an over-the-moon math score on the SAT. Bill's was as high as anyone's could get. He'd gone to Philadelphia and taken a look, but he'd decided on Princeton instead. I was glad for him because he'd treated me as if I belonged in the game even if I wasn't going to be a high scorer.

Lehigh, which was close enough for us to visit if the car was up to a day trip, favored wrestlers. Kinda late for me to qualify as a grappler. Besides, wasn't Lehigh an engineering school? I didn't bother to check how much math I'd have to endure and what other science curses (no, that's not a misspelling) would be stirred into my daily broth. Years later, when I told this tale to my wife, who had been an Ivy Leaguer and whose father had taught at Lehigh, she laughed at my naivete. "The Ivy League is an athletic conference, Bill; there's a range of schools in it, and Penn's not the most selective one." She'd gone to Brown, and she sympathized with me about math courses because Brown had a math requirement. If she'd failed it, she would have had to go to summer school or maybe not graduate. I guess our common disability helped us appreciate one another.

Because we were in the area (and to please my mother), we took a look at the smaller Quaker schools near Philadelphia. We cast only a quick glance at Haverford; my chances of getting in there were thinner than silk. Even a mother with an inflated view of her son's intelligence has realistic moments. A brief look satisfied her. About a week later I heard her tell Isabel Whistler, whose brainy daughter was headed toward a prestigious institution, that I'd looked at Haverford (that's true) and decided against it (not quite true).

At Swarthmore, the glance was even briefer. My father vetoed a longer look because a couple of its graduates had looked down their noses at him. Not the best reason, I know, but I wasn't interested in Swarthmore anyhow. Even if I had been, my chances of getting in there were about as good as winning the Irish Sweepstakes—without a ticket! By summer's end, we hadn't found a school that, for one reason or another, I had a realistic chance of entering.

My senior year at John Harris flew by, accompanied by more mail from more colleges. Some of the schools seemed to be getting desperate. I wondered whether the least of them would still want me if they suspected, as I already did, that I was likely to get a C in chemistry and, if really lucky, a C in trigonometry. So long, National Honor Society.

As the first semester neared its end, bringing with it the time when applications needed to be in the hands of admissions committees, my father hauled me to the kitchen table for a conference. We'd had several uncomfortable sessions in the hot kitchen during the hot summer. That evening's session was basically to eliminate schools my father had put on his list but then found to be too expensive, too snobby, and/ or too damn far away, and others which I simply refused to talk about. We started with a list of six; somehow, without killing one another, we pared the contenders down to two— Dickinson, which would delight my Aunt Marion, a graduate; and Earlham, which would delight my Quaker mother, whose brothers Kenneth and Donald were graduates.

Then my father went one step too far: "Bill," he said, "these here are the applications for Dickinson and Earlham. By this weekend, you gotta fill them out. If you need any help, just ask me."

"No, Pappy, you fill them out. If *you* need any help, *you* ask me. After all, *you're* the one who wants to go."

"Oh, Bob, oh, Bill," my mother moaned.

During track season of my senior year, I ran better times in the mile and the half mile. My coach, Mr. Thomas, had other runners who needed more time than I did, so I could pretty much train at my own pace. I did that, cutting the practice laps in half. It wasn't endurance I needed. Endless laps, my coach's only prescription for distance runners, weren't going to make me any better. Using my version of the program, I saved myself considerable sweat and quite a bit of time. I wasn't just slacking off the way some guys do in the final semester of high school. At the Summer Olympics in July of 1952, Bob Mathias had won the decathlon for the U.S. I'd been avidly following the track and field results from the beginning, with particular interest in how the U.S. would do in the 800 and the 1500, the Olympic versions of the races I'd been running. I'd read that Mal Whitfield of the U.S. had won the 800 meters four years earlier. I was hoping he would repeat. I'd also read that we had a chance for a medal in the 1500. The 1500 came first, and Bob McMillan of the U.S. struck silver, beating the already-famous Roger Bannister, who finished fourth. In the 800, Mal Whitfield did, indeed, repeat.

By the time that race was over, I was totally hooked and gobbling down anything I could read about the track events, including the decathlon. Bob Mathias, the U.S. favorite, got my attention. When the long drawn-out competition was over, Bob Mathias had won. I understood that to do what he'd done, you didn't have to hold the world record in any individual event. You didn't even have to win all of them. It was your all-around performance that counted.

In junior high school, I'd placed third in an athletic contest at the Y. There was a sprint, a standing broad jump, a baseball throw (for accuracy), a medicine ball throw (for distance), a foul shooting contest, and a couple of others that have fled my memory. I won one event, the standing broad jump. But I did well enough in the others (even the ones I can't remember) that I placed third overall. I thought I could do well enough in the running and jumping. I'd like to give the decathlon a shot.

Since I wasn't running endless laps in practice every day, I had some time to try something new. We didn't do the decathlon in high school. Did anyone at any high school do the big ten? I doubt it. But there were guys who threw things. I started to hang out with Coach Schlosser and his discus throwers. I told him that if I went to college, I might try the decathlon. He said that, even in most colleges, the track and field programs didn't include the decathlon; but he encouraged me to work at it, one event at a time. To get started, he suggested I join the workouts with the throwers. I thanked him and said I would. That afternoon Coach Schlosser showed me how to fling the dish, and during what was left of the track season, I practiced with the three guys who did the job for John Harris. I didn't expect to replace any of them, nor did anyone else assume that I would. I was just practicing. Then, a couple of days before our final meet against archrival William Penn, I actually edged out the third of our usual throwers with two of my throws. Mr. Schlosser said, "You know, Bill, if you were a junior, I'd think about entering you in the meet. The fellow you just beat is a junior. He's going to throw."

I said I hadn't expected to throw in the meet. I thanked him, then added, "I was just practicing for next year, if I go to college."

"Bill," he said, "why do you say, '*If* I go to college'? You're a good student. My son, Eddie, says so." (His son Eddie Schlosser was a classmate, a decent athlete, and a better student than I). I gave Coach Schlosser the abbreviated version of my iffiness—that the two schools I'd applied to might be too expensive and that I wasn't sure I wanted to go anyhow.

"Eddie tells me you scored way better than he on the Juniata test. Why not apply there? They have a good track program, and though they don't award athletic scholarships, the fact that you're a good runner could win you financial aid. At least tell your dad about the option."

Mr. Schlosser had been straight with me, so I said I'd talk to my father. That evening, I did. My dad liked the idea. Juniata met all of his criteria. People he respected had graduated from there (and I guess none had looked down a haughty nose at him); the school wasn't too far from Harrisburg for him to drive there and back in a day; and, even without any financial aid, it was significantly cheaper than Dickinson, where I'd been accepted but without any aid. He knew it was late to apply (he'd been reading deadline dates for a year); but he thought we should go see the place. We sent in the papers. I told Mr. Schlosser. He said he'd contact a friend on the coaching staff at Juniata and tell him he thought I could help the school's track team. A couple of days later, Mr. Schlosser's friend called us and told my father we should come for a visit ASAP, preferably the upcoming weekend.

My application hadn't been processed, but the coach told my father he'd hustle it along. A couple of phone calls later, we had an appointment with an admissions officer the following Saturday. Aunt Marion, who had taken a semester off, was already at our house and available for cooking, child-tending for Sister Barbie and Brother Jim, and a dose of manners that could be fun for the latter. Having had trouble civilizing me, she was already mobilizing an early start on him.

We got up early Saturday morning for the trip to Juniata and arrived before noon. Our appointment wasn't until one. My dad said we should scout out the little town of Huntington. It didn't take long. There wasn't much to see. I think that pleased my dad; he remembered my favoring the distractions of Philadelphia. A small-town boy who'd studied to fight off boredom, he favored an ascetic's environment. But I'd grown up in Harrisburg, a fair-sized city with stores and theaters, not only downtown but throughout the residential neighborhoods, three high schools offering games to go to, and a minor league baseball team. This city boy wasn't often bored unless he was forced into the humdrum of homework. Still, we were there. I'd give the place a fair chance to put its best foot forward.

At one o'clock, we met with a dean of admissions; whether he was the only one I don't know. He sat us down in an office and cut right to the chase. If I were admitted (I hadn't been yet, but he thought I would be), he was fairly sure I would be awarded a grant in need of two hundred dollars. The track coach, he said, liked my times. (Thanks, Mr. Schlosser, for telling him I'd placed fourth in both my races in the district meet and, in the half-mile, had beaten William Penn's Hal Swidler, who was being courted by some big-time colleges.) The two hundred bucks had gotten my dad's attention. I could tell he was hooked. *Bye-bye, Dickinson and Earlham,* I thought.

The dean then gave us a tour of the campus, the large dining hall where practically everyone ate, a science building (we didn't go in because the dean had already quizzed me on my interests), the big building where most of the humanities courses met, and the gym. I was interested in gyms, and, as I soon found out, so was my mother. We entered. I checked out the basketball court. My mother exclaimed, "Oh, what a wonderful place for a dance!" What happened next is true; I'd swear on a stack of readable books, even though graduates of Juniata have since denied it. The dean responded to my mother's enthusiasm, "We don't dance at Juniata."

My mother's eyes popped wide open; her mouth formed an exaggerated *O*, making her look like a hungry fish coming straight at dinner. But she uttered not a word. My father, who appeared to be taking in the finer points of the gym's architecture, missed this vignette. The two hundred bucks had caused his eyes to glaze over.

The last stop on the tour was a dormitory, where we were shown a typical freshman room. It looked like a two-person space, but it was set up for three. I later found out that over-loading dorm rooms was typical at small colleges; they were still trying to overcome the enrollment hit delivered by WW II. My attic room at home was looking better and better. I had it all to myself and a double bed to boot. My parents had grown silent in that small space, so I can only imagine what they were thinking. Mother: *how long could such a tiny space contain three boys' dirty laundry?* Father: *at least it's not in the city of distractions.* Me: *If it's hellishly hot in September and June, can I sleep out on the campus?*

The ride back to Harrisburg was entirely silent, except for the roaring motor as Robert D. alternated between too much gas pedal and too little, a habit he'd developed in a jalopy with a slipping clutch that every weekend for sever-al years he'd juked over the mountains from Harrisburg to Wiconisco. The rhythm was sick-making, particularly for Barbie, who, by my mother's good thinking, had been left at home.

Anyone who'd observed and listened to the Keen fami-ly close up would find it difficult to believe we'd ever lived through two hours of silence—not even at a Quaker meet-ing, where at least a couple of the meditators would be moved to speak. But it did happen; silence did prevail on the ride from Huntington to Harrisburg. My father didn't even pause to read historical markers. I'd once quipped to Joe Fiedler and Bill Greenawalt that my dad's car should bear a warning sticker on its bumper: *this car slows down for histori-cal markers.* We'd been tail-ended once, and on several other occasions drivers had screeched past us at the first chance, pumping their fists and uttering unheard threats which must have included every curse in the books.

Believe me, this *was* a silent ride, my father continuing to savor the blessing of a need grant and other advantages of an isolated school. My mother? Her motives were always more complicated than his, but I'd wager that the absence of dancing from the Juniata curriculum was still festering in her heart. Plus, she knew *not* to engage the erratic driver sitting next to her by broaching a controversial subject. Every Keen who'd ever ridden in that car remembered hair-raising experiences of hands off the steering wheel, arms flying wildly, and gas pedal yoyoing from stall to surge.

Back at 2033 we were greeted by Aunt Marion wearing an apron, Barbie half hidden behind her, and Jimmy humming and pounding out a rhythm on the pillows of the davenport. He always was a musical lad. I could smell the vegetable soup. Yum!

My father began to eat. Had the silence on the way home filled the role of grace? My Aunt Marion was a Methodist and favored rhyming-ditty graces. "Bob," she shot forth at her younger brother, thus arresting his soup slurp, "We haven't said grace!"

"Ah, shit…"

"Oh, Bob, language. There are children present," my mother complained.

That was two strikes on Pappy, and we hadn't even gotten to the issue everyone, except Robert D, knew was about to unleash acid indigestion around the table. It was a very old farmhouse table, which in its many residences had served many purposes, including the role of ironing board, for which it, like the one we'd left in Wiconisco, continued to bear the brand of an ancient iron that now did the job of a doorstop. I'd been sitting at a table so branded for years in several locations and had come to think the hot iron brand symbolized the acid reflux that afflicted Keen stomachs when upsetting discussions accompanied the meal.

Sister Barbie got to sound out the grace:

God be with us at the table;
May the food upon the board
Strengthen us and make us able
To work for thee, O Lord.

"Very nice, Barbie," my aunt chimed and, having the floor, like the endless doorbells in Bellevue Park, chimed on, "Gracious, Bob, stop eating; Bill, tell us about your day. What was Juniata like?"

It was Pappy who answered. (Yes, I'd begun to think of him, my dad, my old man, as *Pappy*, because, like L'il Abner's father, he was often beleaguered by a gaggle of strong women.) Pappy said what I knew he had been silently thinking since early that afternoon: "Two hundred dollars…they offered Bill a two-hundred-dollar scholarship to run track!" Already the grant in need had graduated to a more prestigious form.

"Oh, Marion," my mother said. She paused until she had my aunt's full attention, then unleashed her refutation of Pappy's enthusiasm, "They don't dance at Juniata. Can you imagine that, a college where they don't dance?"

"They don't dance? Why not, Enid? What do they do?"

"Yes, they don't dance…for some strange religious reason, I gather, and I, too, wonder what they do instead."

"Aw, for cryin' out loud—" (Pappy watching his language) "—Two hundred dollars a year, and it was already cheaper than Dickinson and Earlham."

"Oh, Bob," sang two female voices, one soprano and one alto. They were ganging up on him. I'd seen it before and I wondered how long it'd be before he forsook his soup and headed for the back porch or lit out on an extended stomp around the neighborhood; but before he could mobilize himself, my aunt stalled any such intention (she'd been there before as well) by asking me what I thought about Juniata.

"I guess it would be OK," I said.

"Just OK, Bill? Can you be more specific? Tell us what you liked about it."

"They have a really good gym."

"You're right, Bill; the gym is well built, very well planned," Pappy piped up.

"But they don't dance in it," my mother countered. She had a nail, and she was going to drive it home.

"What a shame!" my aunt added, then asked, "What else did you like about it?"

"I don't think I have to take math, if I stay with the artsy majors."

"Was there anything you didn't like about it?" My aunt had the floor. She'd gone to years of faculty meetings and had learned how to take control of a discussion and how to hold on to it.

"The dorm rooms are small, and I'd probably be squeezed into one with two other boys. I'd rather stay home where I have a big room all to myself. I could get a job and even pay rent."

"No, Bill; you're going to college. There's a war on over in Korea. You'd be draft bait," Pappy asserted. The two women nodded their agreement. No one at our house ever voted for someone who started a war, even if the government down-played the war by calling it a "police action." Oh, to live in a country that isn't a bellicose aggressor!

"How does Juniata compare to Dickinson?" my aunt asked me.

"I don't know."

"Oh, Bill," my mother said.

"Why don't you know?" my aunt asked.

"I haven't been to Dickinson."

"You haven't been to Dickinson?" she exclaimed.

"No, Marion, he hasn't," my mother said.

"I was gonna take him by now, but then Juniata came up and—"

I interrupted Pappy. "And Mr. Schlosser and the Juniata coach both said we'd better go see the school right away since it was getting late."

"But, Bob," my aunt drove on, "it takes two hours to drive to Huntington; Dickinson is only half an hour away. Surely you could have found the time."

Pappy was getting the worst of it from his sister, her attack reinforced by smiles and knowing nods from my mother. Barbie was staring wide-eyed. Jimmy was humming an agitated tune.

I tried to come to my father's aid: "Pappy did take me to see Dickinson play football down at Hershey last October. That's kind of why I let him apply to Dickinson."

"Because he took you to a football game?" my aunt exclaimed in utter disbelief.

"Yeah. They stunk. They had a 145-pound running back. I'm big enough to play there."

"Oh, Bill," my mother lamented. "How big were the other boys, Bill?"

"Bigger, generally, but they were slow."

"Now, wait once," Pappy blurted out, having caught his breath and located his nerve. "I'm gonna take him to Dickinson—maybe some evening this week. I don't want the boy to decide without seeing both schools."

"What about Earlham? I haven't been there."

"Too far," Pappy whined. " and it's at least as expensive as Dickinson without even considering the travel costs."

"Yeah, and I haven't been accepted."

My mother leaned forward and half rose from her seat as preamble to something: either the meal was over and she was about to clear the plates or she was going to make a speech. Everyone looked at her. You could call it a focusing moment.

"Bill, I know I was the one who suggested Earlham. It's a very good school, and regular contact with the Quakers, with the teachers and the fellow students, and with the people you would meet at meetings, would help you to reach your full potential. And your Uncle Donald and Aunt Jane would be there for moral support. I've tried to show you the way, but without a meeting to help, I haven't entirely succeeded. You've run with some rough boys; you've been in fights; the police have brought you home twice. I've worried that you might end up in White Hill."

"Ah, Enid, he's not been that bad. His grades have been pretty good, mostly A's and B's; just the two C's last semester."

Pappy was actually defending me. That made me feel better.

"May I finish, Bob? He should go see Dickinson; and then we'll…no, then Bill will decide."

"Awright, Enid, awright: if he chooses Dickinson, I'll try to find the money somewhere."

"Bob, will you drive me to Searight's Drugstore? I think we need some Breyers ice cream." Aunt Marion had grown up in a drugstore with a soda fountain. She knew that ice cream could soothe the wounds of battle. When they returned from Searight's with half a gallon of hand-dipped Breyer's featuring scoops of real vanilla beans, my father didn't exactly look happy, but he wasn't hyperventilating either. I guessed he'd accepted the inevitable.

We'd finished eating our dessert, Jimmy and Barbie had been sent upstairs to their room. Aunt Marion and my mother were in the kitchen washing the dishes. Something was afoot.

CHAPTER TEN

A Trip Toward the Future: Father and Son Together

As I had suspected, something was afoot. Barbie and Jimmy were busy playing and Aunt Marion and my mother were scraping, washing, and drying the dishes. My father suggested that he and I take a walk around the block. In a house with too many people, where not even the bathroom was a secure place for private discussions, a usual remedy to overcrowding and eavesdropping was a long walk away from 2033. We strolled along Whitehall toward Twentieth, my father hemming and hawing but not actually getting around to a conversation. We turned to move downhill on Twentieth, and he got rolling.

"Bill, you know Enid and Marion both want you to go to Dickinson, so we'll go to Carlisle and have a look at the school this coming week. Marion wants me to take you during the day, when the offices are open and you might get to talk to a dean. But Gannet, Fleming are caught up in a big water-purification job, and I'm expected to be there all day, every day. We'll have to go in the evening as soon as I get home from work."

"That's OK with me, Pappy."

"Well, there's something else I have to tell you. Your Aunt Marion says she'll pay the difference between Dickinson and Juniata. Much as I'd like to avoid her monkeying in our affairs, she's made the offer. I've thanked her. If you decide to go to Dickinson, she'll be paying part of the cost, so you'll have to thank her too. I understood why you didn't thank her for those manners books she usually gives you at Christmas, but this time, if you decide to go to Dickinson, you'll have to thank her; you'll have to put a smile on and try to sound convincing."

"I'll do my best."

"She doesn't have her own children, you know, so you and Barby and Jim are the substitutes."

"So I've been told."

"Your mother, huh?"

"Yeah."

The following Wednesday evening was to be the day. Pappy thought he could leave work earlier than the usual five-thirty escape time. He hoped we'd be able to stop for fried chicken on the way to Carlisle and still get to the school with plenty of daylight left to illuminate its wonders. That sounded good to me.

On Wednesday, about halfway down Route 11 toward Carlisle, Pappy pulled off the road into the parking lot of a restaurant advertising itself as Slug's Roost.

"This place has great fried chicken, Bill—almost as good as Enid's." My mother's fried chicken, seasoned with a touch of curry powder, had won Pappy over. My grandmother was an excellent cook, but Sunday, chicken day, was also church day in Wiconisco; so the fowl got fixed the easiest way possible, boiling in a big pot along with the potatoes and green beans until everything was a tasteless glop, something on the order of library paste. Years of that gruel caused my father to skip Sunday dinner whenever he could. In Harrisburg, my grandmother had retreated to her bedroom, where she communed with a magazine called the *Upper Room* rather than making her painful arthritic way to a Methodist church.

In recent years, since the ascent of Granma Hannah to the second floor, my mother had done most of the cooking. She fried chicken, and Pappy came back to the table when the fried fowl flew in.

And, according to Pappy, Slug's Roost served great fried chicken—all you could eat of it! Run by a guy who had been an army cook and could provide a large-scale feed trough at a reasonable price, Slug's Roost had won an important place in my father's heart. So we ate and we ate. When I rose to load my plate a third time, Pappy said, "Wait once, Bill: we gotta get on the road or we'll lose the light before you see the campus."

"OK, Pappy," I said. "But we will come back here again, won't we?"

"Hell, yes, Bill, every time we drive you back to school—if you go to Dickinson."

Dickinson one, Juniata zip, I thought. A great meal and no language police around to chant, "Oh, Bob, language, language."

I was impressed by my first drive through Carlisle down Route 11 to the square and, turning right at the old courthouse with the Civil War bullet holes in the columns, on down High Street. Pappy narrated as we drove by but didn't slow down to find an historical marker, because our time to tour before the sun set was limited.

Carlisle was considerably smaller than Harrisburg; but, being the county seat of Cumberland County, it was still bustling at six thirty on a weekday evening. On the first block past the square I spotted the Carlisle Theater, where people stood in line for tickets to *From Here to Eternity*. The film had been to a downtown theater in Harrisburg, but I hadn't seen it yet. I was waiting for a half-price show when it got to the Penway. *Not too shabby*, I thought; *this was definitely not Hicksville*. On the next side street to the right was a busy restaurant, the Hamilton, and, half a block down that street, another movie theater. Dickinson two, Juniata zip! Yeah, I was still trying to decide.

We soon reached the edge of the campus and I began to see gray limestone buildings in a large green space shaded by huge trees, mostly elms. The dreaded Dutch elm disease that, in the 1960s, would bring out noisy chain saws all summer long, was a decade in the future.

We parked out beyond the football field and a second large field which looked as if it would accommodate a second football game. Would there be doubleheaders of helmet-crashers on autumn Saturdays?

Pappy and I walked back to the main campus, passing a frozen custard stand, one more plus for Dickinson. We reached the first fraternity house. It sat proudly at the intersection of High Street and Moreland Avenue. Its columns rose about twenty feet and bore above them its initials in Greek letters. "What's that, Pappy, the BOT house?" I'd studied Latin, but I had no Greek.

Pappy, who'd been in a fraternity at Penn State and had learned the Greek alphabet, corrected me. "Not BOT, Bill; that's Beta Theta Pi."

I was impressed by the columns and said so. My architect father agreed. Our night out had turned into a damn good excursion. Then I spotted what, in retrospect, was probably the deal-sealer.

On the other side of Moreland Avenue was a another green space almost the size of a football field. Unlike the campus we'd driven by coming out from the center of Carlisle, the space was uninterrupted by trees. Two teams of seven guys on a side were engaged in a game of walking football. One of the guys walked the ball around right end. He got a walking block from a lineman. A walking pursuer tagged him after a three-step gain. Then several of the players walked to the sidelines and took turns drinking from a promising-looking pitcher. "Looks like a loving cup," Pappy said.

"Hunh?"

"A loving cup. Fraternities use them in ceremonies, usually filled with wine, but I'm guessing, from the rate they're guzzling it down, that one's filled with beer."

They lined up again and walked a passing play. A defender made a walking interception. He walked to the sideline and hoisted the cup. I didn't think the game would last very long.

"Your mother wouldn't mind if you played that kind of football," Pappy said, "but she'd want you to stay away from the pitcher."

"Yeah, you're probably right," I said. It was about then that I knew I knew, so after a moment's rumination, I added, "Pappy, I'm glad we did this." I had decided in the way a lot of young jerks decided things in those days, a glimpse of a bunch of guys in college actually having fun—something to offset the overload of seriousness I'd felt for the past two years.

From the Beta Theta Pi fraternity house, Dickinson ran two long city blocks back toward the center of Carlisle, and it looked to be almost as wide as it was long. We came upon other fraternity houses. "Alpha Chi Rho, Theta Chi, Phi Kappa Psi," my father translated as we passed each one.

"Geez," I said, "that's a lot of fraternities."

"Ten nationals," he said.

"How do you know? Have you visited here before?"

"Oh, yeah, Bill, I've been to Carlisle a number of times, when Marion graduated and since then for Clayton Lappley and Gannett, Fleming, taking measurements for remodeling jobs. But I've known about fraternities for a long time. I was a charter member of Triangle at Penn State. We had dances, and I invited Enid Parker to come to a spring weekend and dance with me."

"Is that where the scarab came from?" I asked. On the wall next to the clothes closet at 2033 there was a wooden abstract of a scarab. I knew my father had made it in college in order to be initiated into some organization, but I'd assumed it was a more academic group for people good in math and science, not one to which he'd taken a blind date from Harrisburg before they'd married and become my parents.

There was a bench. We sat on it, and my father told me how he and my mother had met; and about the Triangle Fraternity, which was a serious group of engineering students; and about the scarab, which, like an architect, was a builder; and about the car he drove from Penn State to the

Clark's Ferry Bridge to meet the blind date a fraternity brother had arranged for him; and how, back at Penn State, they had danced and they had danced. "So I've known something about fraternities since my college days; but I also read the material Dickinson sent you. Now that you may be coming here, you should read it too. Start with the catalog. Come on, right now we better walk; it'll be getting dark soon." I looked back the way we'd come. It was too far to see the walking players, but I guessed they had walked away.

At the corner past Phi Kappa Psi , we saw a Methodist church and, catty-cornered from it, a large brownstone building that took up half a block of the street that ran into High Street. "That's the main classroom building for pretty much everything except the sciences," Pappy said. "It's called Denny Hall. I think that's where they hold English classes and history."

As if it had heard its name called, a historical marker popped up. Pappy read it: "Look, Bill, on this spot George Washington reviewed the troops before marching west to quell the Whiskey Rebellion going on in Washington, Pennsylvania, out near Pittsburgh."

He identified another, newer-looking fraternity house located on the same side of the street and just across an alley from the big classroom building: "That's Phi Delta Theta. There's a Sigma Chi chapter too, but I think the house is up a side street, so we missed it. Dickinson has the whole Miami

Triad, this one, Sigma Chi, and the first one we saw, Beta Theta Pi."

"Why are they the Miami Triad, Pappy?

"The three of them were founded at Miami University out in Ohio. When all three have chapters at a school, they usually have a weekend with lots of dancing. If you joined Phi Delta Theta your mother might actually shed a tear."

"How come?"

"It's a long story, Bill. And it's getting dark. C'mon, there're two more buildings I want to show you."

We crossed the street and entered the large yard we'd driven by before, the one with the collection of limestone buildings under a roof of huge elm trees. We entered a gate where once upon a time a black man named Noah Pinckney had sold "Dickinson sandwiches" to students. We stopped in front of the first building, a substantial multistoried limestone building that looked about as old and established as the limestone farmhouses we'd driven past on Route 11 on our way to Carlisle. Pappy, standing in as a historical marker, declared, "This is East College, the oldest college dormitory west of the Susquehanna." He'd read the catalog.

As we walked along the front of East College, I wondered whether I'd ever live in the revered dormitory. If I did, I'd have bragging rights at parties that John Harris classmates headed to the Ivies might attend. Yeah, I know, it sounds stupid; but this was all new to me. I hadn't begun to be selective, to make intelligent choices from among competing possibilities. Hell, I'm still having trouble doing that.

Pappy glanced toward a row of older buildings back behind East College. "Those are science buildings, Bill; considering your C in chemistry last semester, you'd better stay away from them."

"I'll do my best, Pappy," I replied. But I hadn't yet read the catalog.

We stopped in front of the stone stairs leading up to the entrance of another limestone building, a more impressive one even than the revered East College. Pappy bowed his head. He looked like he was going to pray.

"This grand building," my father intoned in an almost preacherly way, "Is Old West College, the most famous college building west of the Susquehanna." I was beginning to wonder if there was some special category of American architectural history called "Buildings west of the Susquehanna." Apparently Pappy thought so. It looked like he was warming up for a longer dissertation: but it was getting dark, so he cut it short. "It was designed by Benjamin Latrobe, the most famous American architect of his time, the early nineteenth century. We read about it in a history of architecture when I was in school."

"Latrobe," my father continued, "designed the capitol in Washington and a lot of other buildings, even a prison in Virginia. He brought back classical forms to architecture. I tried to work in the same way when I was designing houses for Shimmel and Binder in Country Club Hills." I knew that the Country Club Hills period, when Pappy had designed houses for people to live in, had been the happiest time in his career. I also knew that the job had lasted for only a couple of years. After that, he'd bitten the bullet and done public works projects, remodeling an exercise yard for patients at Danville and designing any number of sewage disposal plants—though, as far as I knew, never a prison. I guess architects, particularly the not-famous ones, have got to take what they can get.

It was nearly dark then. Pappy said, "That other limestone building right over there," pointing at it, "is Bosler Hall. It houses the college library and the chapel. If you come here, you'll find out about it in September." He'd read the catalog. I knew that, when I got home, I'd begin to read it too. I was coming to Dickinson.

CARLISLE

CHAPTER ONE

Joining the Singing:
"Each Ancient Classic Wall"

On July 27, 1953, the Korean War came to an end, thus canceling the primary reason I'd listened to the mantra of parents and teachers about going to college; I was between a rock and a hard place, which is only better than being between a gray sky and a sodden place. I hadn't wanted to go to college, but now I'd visited Carlisle with my father on one of the longest outings alone with him that I could remember; and I'd been affected by his enthusiasm for fraternities and history and beautiful old buildings. For the first time since he'd started to influence me, like soft dough that still needed work, I felt I owed him something. Maybe I'd actually turn out to be a pretzel. That and mustard and a beer might make the whole process worthwhile.

As we walked back through the campus to where we'd parked the car, neither of us talked much. When we got to

the now-deserted field where we'd watched the walking football game, I said, "Beta Theta Pi."

"That's right, Bill, Beta Theta Pi. One of the Miami Triad
fraternities," he replied. I told myself that when I got to
school in the fall, I'd visit that one.

Arriving back home, we found everyone gathered in the
living room. It was late, but my sibs were still up; even my
grandmother had come downstairs for the showdown. I cut
right to the chase: "I'm going to Dickinson." My mother
smiled; Aunt Marion bobbed her head vigorously; Sister
Barbie clapped her hands and squealed; Brother Jim began
to play his rhythm game on the arm of a chair; and Pappy
slapped me on the back. They were happy, and I was glad I'd
made them happy. Most of all, I was glad that Pappy, the constant worrier about money, wanted me to go to Dickinson.

I'd begun to guess Dickinson was his preference, though
he'd never actually said so. Did a Benjamin Latrobe building trump a new gym? And what led me to think he was
rooting for Dickinson? I guess I didn't actually know, but
I had sensed from his enthusiasm as he guided me through
the tour that he thought it was the place for me. He'd often
said I shouldn't follow in his footsteps to Penn State, but I
thought that was because he feared I'd be swallowed by the
place; and I sometimes wondered if he'd been threatened by
its size—he was a small-town boy. I guess I'll never know
for sure, because he never said anything about it. He could

be emotional, erupting over some nasty thing that had been said about or done to someone he respected, but he seldom explained his feelings.

What he did say was that he hadn't entered college right away. His father, he told me, had decided to support not only his own children but at least one other deserving person. When Aunt Marion was a senior at Dickinson, George Keen had paid the bill for a young woman, known to me only as Rosalie, for the two-year teacher-preparation program at Shippensburg. The year my aunt graduated from Dickinson, Rosalie still had one more year to go. My father was slowed down by his father's generosity. Already out of high school, he couldn't start college "on time," so he stayed home in Wiconisco, helping out in the pharmacy and pumping gas for the cars that were beginning to disrupt the peace.

Pappy's talk about this delay (which I heard more than once) seemed to me a mixture of complaint and relief: he was eager to begin but afraid he wasn't ready: "You know, Bill, I was born on October 23. Like you, I was only seventeen when I graduated from high school, and I was going into architectural engineering, one of the toughest courses at State, lots of math and physics."

I knew I'd be safe from the math demon, but I probably should have asked myself whether I was up to some of the other challenges, particularly the endless list of required courses I'd read about in the catalog. But I didn't. I hung out with my friends and played as much basketball as I could get in each evening. The most popular song during my time at John Harris had been Nat King Cole's version of "Too Young"—not just too young to be in love. How about too young to go to college? But I hadn't heard anyone singing that version. High school hadn't been easy, but I seldom had homework in more than two classes.

Several nights after the Dickinson jaunt, I found myself in a familiar place, the catechism chair, my back up against the silverware drawer. I think my mother saw her chances of licking her oldest cub into shape fast fading away. She washed dishes. I waited. "I'm glad you'll be going to Dickinson, Bill. It's the right place for you. And it's close enough that we can drive over and see you."

I wasn't sure how I felt about that—sort of like a yo-yo on a short string, maybe—but I kept the thought to myself. "Pappy really got into the fraternity thing," I said to change the direction of our talk.

"Oh, yes, Bill, he was very proud he'd been a charter member of Triangle at Penn State."

"He identified all the houses we walked by and went on about the three founded at Miami in Ohio. He said he thought you'd be pleased if I joined Phi Delta Theta. Would that please you?"

"Oh, I suppose so…yes, it would!"

"Why?"

"A boy from Richmond who was a friend of mine during high school was in Phi Delta Theta at Miami."

"A boyfriend?"

"No, Bill, a boy who was a friend in high school. He was my best girlfriend's boyfriend. I tutored him in Spanish so he could raise his grade. He was a good athlete in high school and at Miami. He later became a well-known football coach."

"What was his name?"

"Weeb Eubank."

"Oh, yeah, I've heard of him."

I looked at my mother. She seemed to be crying. Maybe she'd gotten dish soap in her eyes.

Late in August, emanations from Dickinson began to complicate my feelings. The first to arrive through the mail slot was a list of my fall-semester courses. Someone in Carlisle had decided I needed to take psychology, history, English, and French. I would also be asked to choose between physical education and ROTC. The first three seemed fine to me. I'd not had psychology in high school. It wasn't offered—unless it was hiding out in one of the civics courses I hadn't taken. I'd done well in history and English (mostly A's); I figured they'd be manageable. But why French? Why couldn't I take more Latin, my favorite course in high school? I decided I'd ask that question again. The last course, the choice of either physical education or ROTC, was easy enough: I'd always enjoyed gym class.

My mother looked at the list and said nothing. When Pappy came home that evening, I showed him the list. He read it, looked at my mother, and said in a flat voice, "He's not taking French." Those were his exact words.

For once she didn't say, "Oh, Bob." She didn't say anything.

Again, my father said, "He's not taking French." Again, his exact words. Some things said are simply remembered.

"Right, Pappy, I don't want to take French," I said, adding, in more or less these words, "Why can't I take more Latin? Isn't college where you go to study subjects you're interested in? I'm interested in Latin, and they teach Latin at Dickinson." I knew that because I'd started to read the catalog.

What I didn't know was why Pappy was so opposed to French. Maybe I should have been able to figure out why; but I hadn't then, and I wouldn't begin to understand until I was out of college, had read a lot more history, and had traveled in Europe. My father never got to Europe, never saw the Acropolis, never visited Alsace-Lorraine, Switzerland, or the Palatinate; but he'd gone to the state library and he'd read the history he'd not had time to study in the science-ridden curriculum at Penn State. He knew how the French had treated his ancestors. I now know, having studied French, German, and Italian, that you shouldn't hate a language because of the wars its speakers wage. But I can also understand why my dad didn't want me to take French.

As I recall, that conversation about what I'd be taking concluded with my mother saying that schedules could be changed and my father proclaiming that mine would be changed to some other language and adding that I should take ROTC. And then the evening concluded along these lines.

"Why, Bob? Why not physical education?"

"Enid, you're the Quaker: you're the one who doesn't want him in the military. I know, I know, the Korean War is over; but there's still a draft, and by taking ROTC he can avoid the draft for a while and go in as an officer."

"But, Bob, he shouldn't have to go in at all."

"Enid, the boy's got to serve his country; and as far as I can tell, he's not a conscientious objector."

"No, he's not: but there must be other ways to serve his country than by killing other people." Damn. Going to college—all it does is eat up your time with more questions.

Around lunchtime the following day, I got a phone call from a Dickinson student who said he'd like to come to the house, talk to me about school, and answer any questions I might have. We'd just finished supper when he appeared with a second guy in tow whom he introduced as his fraternity brother. They talked very generally about the college, and then got down to the real business, the importance of fraternities in providing big brotherly advice to freshmen and a social life at Dickinson.

I asked him about my schedule: did he think I'd be able to take Latin instead of French? He hemmed and hawed, apparently knowing more about his fraternity than the courses. He clearly hadn't read the catalog recently. I went into my escape mode, perfected through twelve years of intermittent boredom in the public schools and particularly useful in enduring church services and sales pitches. My father filled in for me, loving the fraternity chatter and even threatening to sing the song associated with our visitors' national.

"Oh, Bob," my mother said, scotching his musical effort in the bud.

A couple of evenings later, I was visited by another Dickinson student who'd called asking to visit and answer my questions about the college. My father said it was another fraternity man, trying to get a head start on rushing. I asked Pappy what *rushing* was; it seemed a bit threatening to me. After all, I was being rushed into college; I didn't think I needed any more forces hustling me along.

John Winand was older than the other fraternity guys had been. He'd been in the military, the navy, I think. He'd finished his tour the year before, just in time to enter Dickinson on the GI Bill. He'd be a sophomore in the fall: and, what do you think, he'd be going out for football! We had something to talk about. He'd also brushed up his knowledge of the catalog. Yes, I'd be able to change my schedule. Possibly, I'd be able to take Latin, if the one teacher was offering an advanced course. Yes, ROTC was a good way to delay the draft; besides, the phys ed courses didn't amount to much.

John Winand had graduated from John Harris. We talked about some of the teachers we'd both had. It was almost as an afterthought that he identified himself as a member of Beta Theta Pi, adding that he hoped I'd stop over to the house when I got to campus. He was beginning to tell me where it was located when I interrupted him.

"I know where it is; my dad took me over to Carlisle and pointed out lots of buildings, including the Beta Theta Pi house." Remembering the walking football game Pappy and I had come upon that evening, I said I'd be sure to visit it.

CHAPTER TWO

Appearance? Reality?:
Beyond the Point of No Return

Saturday, September 12, 1953, was a cloudy day. Showers were expected. I don't remember whether they actually occurred. And I didn't yet know that Carlisle, having more than its share of rainy days, bore the nickname *Drizzly Carlizzly.* During my years there I often wondered if it rained as much in Huntington, Pennsylvania. Also, I did not know that I was subject to depression caused by a lack of sunlight, thanks to the Swedes and Germans who were my European ancestors. Back then, I don't think any layman knew much about this SAD condition, though something was going on among my folks who often talked of the *mully-grubbs* and griped about being *down in the dumps.*

Even if I had known how much my soul craved sunlight, going to school where Old Sol actually shone on most days of the year was way beyond the limit of my parents' distance allowance. So, there I was in Drizzly Carlizzly but not at all convinced I'd be there very long. The likelihood of my failing and being drafted was very high. Maybe it would be to a place where the sun was on full duty and I could be gunned down with a smile on my face.

Near the end of the first semester, I was experiencing what I now know was depression. The cause was not just the weather. I was also convinced I shouldn't be at Dickinson and maybe not anywhere in the holy groves. The list of courses I'd been faced with in the first year was more than I could manage.

Despite the cloudiness of that first day, however, I remember it starting out as a positive experience. We, my mother, my father, and I, left Harrisburg early that morning. Barbie and Jimmie stayed at home under the supervision of Aunt Marion. The three of us arrived in Carlisle and went directly to the famous old building. Pappy was in his element. Instead of joining the line where he'd have to pay up to get me started, he dragged me to an upper floor, found an open classroom, and launched into a lecture on its random width flooring, which, he proclaimed, authenticated Old West's antiquity. Then he paid the bill and asked if it would be possible to change the schedule I'd been sent. We were assured that some changes would be possible. That afternoon I was to meet with my advisor, Mrs. Ramos. She would help me make the changes.

I don't remember lunch, which must have been some kind of omen. Pennsylvania Germans aren't likely to forget their meals. After we'd eaten whatever it was we'd eaten, we found Mrs. Ramos's office in Denny Hall. She was a pleasant-looking, smiling, white-haired lady. My mother greeted her in Spanish (a good guess) and they seemed immediately to be fast friends. My father hemmed and hawed a bit, then brought up the issue of a schedule change. "Bill's been signed up for French; he's not taking French."

Mrs. Ramos asked me, "What language would you like to take, Bill?"

"Latin," I replied. "I've had three years in high school; it was my favorite subject."

It wasn't to be. Short version: I'd had more Latin than was being offered that semester. I shouldn't wait until my sophomore year to start a language; but Latin, Mrs. Ramos assured me, would help me with Spanish. My mother and Mrs. Ramos exchanged smiles about the Spanish; my father said, "Spanish is OK." I chalked up one disappointment: no Latin.

Pappy asked about ROTC. Mrs. Ramos directed us to the basement of Denny Hall, where we found Col. Rachel, the head of Dickinson's program. He agreed with my father that ROTC would be a good choice for keeping me in college and out of the draft. I know my mother was distressed by the idea, but she didn't speak up. The basic program was for

two years, the colonel explained: it would satisfy the physical education requirement. I asked the colonel if I could try
ROTC for a year, and, if it wasn't for me, switch to physical
education for the second year. He told me the switch was
possible. So that was it: Spanish, ROTC, psychology, history,
and freshman English.

After that, we found Conway Hall. We lugged my stuff
up to the fourth floor (fortunately, I didn't have much) and
installed me in a huge room, a lot bigger than the room I'd
been shown at Juniata. It had three beds in it, and they'd been
there for a while. Pappy inspected the springs and declared
they were shot; he'd bring a piece of plywood to shore up
the sagging springs later in the week. Unfortunately, Gannet,
Fleming roared into a new job, a sewage disposal plant somewhere up the Susquehanna, and the springs sagged for several weeks. By that time, my back was bothering me, and
for that reason, my freshman football career at Dickinson
had come to an end. It probably wouldn't have lasted much
longer anyhow, because by the end of one week of classes I
knew I was in trouble.

Let's get this over as quickly as possible. I shouldn't have
been accepted by Dickinson College. If anyone had paid attention to me, I wouldn't have been. But no one at the college did. I was never interviewed, unless we count the visits
from fraternity guys as interviews. I was never invited to visit the campus. My father applied. I was accepted. Why did

they take me? Here are my guesses. Dickinson needed paying bodies. Several of my relatives had graduated from the
school. I'd had decent but not super grades at a high school
from which Dickinson regularly accepted quite a few students. In my year there were only two of us—Miles Gibbons,
a better student at John Harris than I, was the other one—
but in most years there had been three or four, most of them
National Honor Society members. For me, the society had
been a near miss, but, bottom line, I wasn't a member.

My career at Dickinson College, even before I stepped
into my first classroom, had gotten off to a *really bad start*. As
I write this, I remember Ed Sullivan beginning the Tonight
Show with his promise of a *really big show*. The first meeting
of the class of 1957 took place in Bosler Hall at 7 p.m. on
Sunday, September 13. It was a *really bad show*.

A first-page article in the *Carlisle Sentinel* for Monday,
September 14, 1953, discusses the opening assembly for
the two hundred and forty new students in positive terms.
President Edel had told us we were "now part of 'a long
procession'" that had included "some of the great men and
women of America."[1] At any rate, that's what the article said;
but I don't remember. I probably blocked it out as yet another preachment about my responsibility to keep things going.
He also said the college was "a community of learners" in
which "students and teachers alike are dedicated to the search
for the truth" and assured us that there was "room for the

---

1   *Carlisle Sentinel,* Monday, September 14, 1953, p.1

new student" who "made this search his first objective and remained strong in his own individuality." Edel proclaimed, "Dickinson makes no robots." The praise of individuality and the disdain for robots, I do remember.

What I remember most clearly was Dean Frederick Ness instructing each of us to look to the right and to the left and to bear in mind that at least one of the three in our glancing group wouldn't be here very long. The dean seemed proud of the college's capacity to flunk out one in three. Figuring he was talking about me, right then I began to think of myself as the weed to be plucked. Since then, in sharing this frighten-the-frosh tactic with others of my age group, I've discovered that lots of new students at lots of colleges received the same jolting message. Apparently deans went to conferences where they were schooled in how to scare the shit out of new students. Well, it worked on me. I guess deans are allowed to be robots.

I remember vowing to myself to stay as far away from Dean Ness as was humanly possible. That worked until the second semester of my senior year (more about that later). Yeah, I wasn't one of the three who wasn't going to hang around. I lasted because I was lucky: I soon discovered what wasn't for me and what was. You could call it the alternative curriculum.

Oh, yes, I remember one more thing from that first convocation: the words on the wall. No, not "Mene mene tekel upharsin" (though the way I was feeling, they would have been appropriate). And, yeah, I did know about the hand-writing on the wall—I'd spent more than enough days in Sunday school being told about the misfortunes hiding in the shadows not very far down the road. Rather, the words on the wall in the chapel of Bosler Hall proclaimed,

This is the Chapel: here, my son,

Your father thought the thoughts of youth,

And heard the words that one by one

The touch of Life has turned to truth...

I wrote them down so that I could look them up. A couple days later, I went back to Bosler Hall, which also housed the college library, and, with the help of a librarian, found the poem, "Clifton Chapel" by Henry Newbolt, and read it, finding there its suggestion that I "might speak with noble ghosts/Of manhood and the vows of war" and that I might "count the life of battle good" and contemplate "the frontier-grave" so "far away." And there I was, signed up for ROTC. Someone, I thought, is pulling my strings.

CHAPTER THREE

Endless Reading and Vomiting Mailboxes: Diverging Tracks in the College Woods

Before I could enter the alternative curriculum, I spent a wearying time trying to do my best with that part of the prescribed one assigned to me. Let's clear away the sources of the dismal beginning so I can get beyond it to more positive features of my first year.

First source: Misrepresentation—first semester Spanish is for beginners. I and one or two others in the class were beginners. Most of the class, I soon discovered, had had Spanish in prep school. They were beginning over again; why couldn't I have taken Latin? I could have, indeed, by agreeing to read beyond the texts of first-year Latin, a fact I discovered too late to act on it. I guess Mrs. Ramos didn't know that; then again, she was a Spanish teacher.

Second source: More misrepresentation? No, let's call it "Not Yet Knowing How to Hear What Was Almost Not

Said." Col. Rachel had said that the basic program in ROTC was for two years; but he also said I could switch to phys ed after one year. Later on, when I tried to do that, he told me the cost: I'd lose credit for the year I'd spent in ROTC. Why? The basic course was a hyphenated two-year sequence, not a batch of comma courses. Shit! Done in by punctuation. Still seems like bait and switch to me.

Third source: Teacher's Expectations vs. the Reality of Student's Preparation—world history. The class featured reading assignments of about twenty pages an evening. Each sentence presented me with two or three new facts to be memorized. After two days, I was drowning. I began to search for the teacher; I found his office but not him. On the third day I screwed my courage to the bubblegum point, approached him in the classroom, and asked if he could show me how to read a history book. He told me to see him after class. I did. The gist of that meeting was that I should have learned how to read a history book in prep school.

The question forming in my mind was: should I leave Dickinson and go to a prep school? I didn't ask the question. I already knew the answer. Hell, I'd been there over a week, and I'd heard countless comments by prep school graduates that "this course was a snap because we already did this and that in prep school. This course was a piece of cake…" Yeah, prep school again. One guy even said his prep school sent so many students to Dickinson that they had files on the teachers here. He'd been advised to use the files and to avoid anyone new.

I said to myself—the teachers want students who have been to prep school, but the college is admitting all kinds of warm bodies who haven't been. Maybe the admissions people hadn't told the teachers. That led me to a new reading of Dean Ness's look to the right, look to the left: if you're not a prep school student, we'll take your family's money for a year; then most likely you'll be the one in three who'll be gone. I didn't know how I was going to survive. Though I was learning to hate the place, I'd be damned if I'd let them flunk me out of it. The competitive spirit which had allowed me to be lured into races I wasn't eager to run was fiddling me in another way, and I was too green to escape the binding of soul by its own spirit.

First semester was complicated by several other forces in motion. Given the high tonality of the word bath that had been sprayed on us at the first convocation, these currents seemed like non sequiturs. At the very least, the administration and the faculty weren't holding hands, and no one was holding hands with the self-appointed student leaders, an uppity lot who needed to be restrained.

No robots at Dickinson? Hmm. Early meeting with dorm proctors: assignments—at the bookstore, buy a beanie and wear it; buy a twelve-by-twelve-inch piece of cardboard, print your name on it, add a string, and wear the sign around your neck. Memorize the Dickinson songs and cheers. Always carry the Dickinson Handbook. Carry matches at all times; light the gasper of any upper-class student who applies to you for a nicotine fix. No, you don't have to furnish the cigarette. Know the names of all the White Hats and all the Black Hats. Be back in the dorm by nine every night Sundays through Thursdays. Be ready to go out on punishment detail on Wednesday nights. When are we supposed to study?

Study? Forget it until rushing is over. First week or so is stuff you already know from prep school. Prep school? That's a laugh. And ah, yes, rushing. Pappy had said I should go through the rushing program, which meant making the rounds for meals (breakfast, lunch, and dinner) at each of the ten fraternities—one fraternity Monday, a second one Tuesday, etc., etc.—if for no other reason than to find out which house had the best cook. I made the rounds and discovered a steady diet of hot dogs and baked beans for lunch and banquet meat pies for dinner; fish sticks on Friday night. I usually skipped breakfast. At the meals I went to, I shook a lot of hands, answered "I don't know" to repeated questions about my prospective major, and proclaimed "no thanks, I don't smoke" to multiple offers.

Each afternoon when I returned from classes, I'd join the crowd at the mailboxes in Conway Hall and unload a hoard of envelopes inviting me to spend the evening at this and that fraternity's "smoker." I dumped them in the wastebasket, climbed the stairs to the fourth floor and tried to read the history assignment. If my roommate, Sherwood Powers, was there, he'd ask me what smokers I'd been invited to that evening and which ones I'd be going to. "Probably none of them," I'd say.

We'd natter on at one another, I insisting that even at lunch and dinner I'd leave the designated fraternity with burning eyes—he warning that, if I didn't meet the brothers, I might not get a bid and reminding me that there wasn't anything to do here if you weren't in a fraternity. He was probably right. We heard the same thing from the brothers at lunch and dinner every day. Sherwood and almost everyone else was playing the game; and I was pretty sure he thought I was stupid or a snob because I wasn't. I didn't think I was a snob, but maybe I was stupid. He was headed to Theta Chi, his first choice. I liked the guys I'd met there at meals. A lot of them were athletes. Many of them didn't smoke. I had something to talk about, and my eyes didn't burn so much. Still, I needed to read my history assignment.

One of the new programs at Dickinson in 1953 was the dorm resident program. For the lot of us living in Conway Hall, there were upperclassmen who were supposed to help us adjust to college. Sherwood and I were in a group of twenty or so who'd been installed in rooms in the front half of the fourth floor. Our student counselor, Warren Harrop, lived in the room right next to Sherwood and me.

One evening when Sherwood had gone to a smoker and I was fighting with the history book, our counselor knocked on our door. I invited him in; and after some small talk, he got around to the reason for his visit. He knew I wasn't going to the smokers and he wondered why. I gave him my reason: eye pain from smoke and trying to read history. Hadn't John Winand visited me during the summer and invited me to stop in at the Beta house? Yes to both. Why hadn't I stopped by the house? Well, I'd eaten there, but I hadn't seen John Winand. Warren asked me to join him that evening. We'd find a place in the house away from the smokers, and he'd introduce me to an A student in history. So we went across the street to the Beta house. I heard the piano and the singing as soon as we got there. Eight or ten guys were gathered around the piano singing "Ain't She Sweet." I knew the words. I joined in. When we'd finished the song, the piano player stood up, stuck out his hand, and said, "I'm Jay Hughes; and who is this freshman who knows how to sing?"

"Bill Keen."

"Bill Keen...from Harrisburg...John Winand visited you...where've you been?"

"Mostly over in Conway."

"Conway? There's no piano in Conway."

"Yeah, I was beginning to think there weren't any pianos or singers at Dickinson—just smokers."

"There are a lot of smokers; but in this house there are two pianos, and three piano players; and that man you were just harmonizing with…"

"Hello, Bill; I'm Bob Hoover." He stuck out his hand. I shook it. "I'm vice president of the glee club. You should try out." I said I would. We sang "Five Foot Two," another song I knew.

"We know some of the same songs, Bill; where'd you learn them?" Bob Hoover asked.

"At home. My father plays them on the piano."

Then I was invited to a party the following Saturday night with the promise that there'd be lots of singing. I said I'd show up. It was turning into a productive evening, and it wasn't over yet.

Warren Harrop took me aside and introduced me to Tom Hough, who was a top history student. Tom Hough asked me what the problem was. I told him the book was so packed with facts I couldn't sort out the most important ones. He recommended an outline book that would help me do that. I should read the outline book first; then go back to the textbook and pick out some details for each point in the outline. Those are the important points. The outline book would explain why. "Thanks, Tom; where'd you learn this?"

"Sewickley Academy."

I should have known.

By semester's end, I was feeling more comfortable at Dickinson. I'd joined seven other guys from my class as pledges of Beta Theta Pi. (Yeah, I know, it was a lilly-white frat—Dickinson was lily-white. But they had included me, and it felt good to be included.) I'd tried out for and been accepted into the men's glee club. I'd started for the Beta tag football team and scored a couple of touchdowns; we'd won most of our games. I'd waited on tables at the Beta house, thus cutting the cost of my food; and I'd earned some spending money by helping Ross Brown and John Winand in the sandwich business. And my grades, though not world-beating, were good enough that my overall average was above 2.00. I would soon become a brother of Beta Theta Pi. Hey, here's the skinny on it: I'd been introduced to the alternative curriculum. Very little of it had anything to do with what was in the catalog. I could see the possibility of learning a lot at Dickinson. Most of it wouldn't be in the classroom.

But you've got to satisfy the requirements of the classrooms to graduate. That means you'll have to pass required courses (thankfully not math!); others where you'll have some choice; and courses in a major, in which, presumably, you have something (talent or interest or maybe both) going for you. Man, there were endless classrooms! The basic course of the alternative curriculum is to scout out the teachers who own these classrooms. You need to find out whom to avoid—and believe me, there are

teachers to avoid; in any school ever imagined or established, there are teachers to avoid. There are the brilliant
ones who can't allow that any young punk could come up
with an idea worth considering; if you put it in a paper,
they'll say you plagiarized it. There are ones with visions
of their own productive ability who husband their time so
tightly a student in need can never find them. There are
downright lazy ones and ones so scared of the world that
they've sought protective custody in academe. These sorts
are better at hibernating than a well-fed bear. There are
lechers, hungry for young bodies of any sexual persuasion.
And, now, since the stupidity of anti-age discrimination
has been extended to allow tenured teachers to stay on
forever—that is, until they're toted out of classroom or
lab or office—out of wherever they might be hiding or hibernating—in a wooden box, there are the immortals. In
bad times, when new hires are rare, these Struldbrugs have
the effect of slowing new blood and energy and ideas from
entering the academy until progress in higher education
freezes to a standstill, like a jar of molasses left out in a
winter storm—somewhere near Oswego.

How do you sort out the winners from the losers? And,
believe me, there are winners. The time you invest in finding
them is well spent. How do you do this? Listen a lot. Back
in the fifties at Dickinson, there were good places for listening—the dorms, the fraternities, and South College.

South College was left over from army use of the college during World War II—sort of like a barracks; by God, it might have been a barracks! It was full of round tables that would accommodate a lot of chairs and coffee cups. It had a snack bar where, in 1953, you could get a cup of coffee for a nickel; and it was close to classrooms in Denny, the library, the gym, and several of the fraternity houses. You could enter, get coffee—even I could afford a couple cups a day—squeeze in around a well-populated table, and listen. If you'd already heard your fraternity brothers talking about teachers, at South College you could broaden your view by listening to a great variety of students, including many of the wise and good-looking women who seemed to live in South College.

I often wondered why the upperclasswomen who lived in nearby Drayer spent so much time at South College. Was the dorm not heated or badly ventilated? I could understand why the first-year women flocked to South between classes. It was a mile or more back to Metzger and Gibbs where they were housed. But Drayer was right near the center of activities. So, one day when I was having coffee with a junior woman who was easy to talk to, and, uncharacteristically, we had a large table to ourselves, I asked her why the women from Drayer spent so much time in South, the dorm being just a block away.

"Oh, Bill," she said, "they lock us up in Drayer from ten fifteen at night until just before classes in the morning. South is like being on parole." Then she added, "Besides, in South, we get to talk to cute little boys like you, who aren't yet all full of themselves, like their big-deal fraternity brothers." I blushed. Then I smiled because I'd asked. I'd remember.

Once you hear something that sounds true, remember it. Then, as soon as possible, write it down. Every evening before you zonk out, or earlier if there's time, go through the scribblings and organize what folks have said about particular teachers. Use that information when you register, and go back and review it when you've developed your own opinion. Listen, take notes, organize, and reconsider. This is a basic method of the alternative curriculum. It works most of the time. And, you know what? A version of this process works for classes too. Think about it.

If no clear recommendation arises right away, keep on asking other experienced students. And, oh, yeah, when you have some experience of the teachers, check your notes to see which students gave you good advice. Takes a lot of time, but that's the way it is with real living and real learning. And you know, because I was actively involved in doing it, I never had to memorize the results.

In the best of all possible worlds, the teachers themselves will be part of this advising process; but as far as I could tell, Dickinson in 1953 was not the best of all possible worlds, at least not until you chose your major. In the major you had some idea which teachers might give you good advice because you'd taken courses from them. In all fairness to my teachers, there were ones who tried to give students good advice. There was even a movement to foreground advising as a faculty responsibility, but it hadn't really taken off. I don't know why for certain, but I'd guess that there hadn't been a faculty and staff conversation about who the students were, how many of them hadn't had the advantage of a prep school education, and what kinds of courses might help them learn how to read the books of the various disciplines—students like me who didn't know how to read the history book but could have learned how if someone had given a damn.

There were many problems at Dickinson in the 1950s—none more severe, I think, than unresolved issues of the college's purpose that brought competing forces to explosive conclusions in 1957. More about that later.

Was I a successful student? At the time, if you remained a C to C-plus student and didn't fail any courses, you could stay in college. I never failed a course; I stayed in college. And in my senior year, I actually became a B student, helped along by the one and only A of my Dickinson career.

I actually did benefit from a number of my teachers, most of them in the English department. There were two others, not in the English department. I'll start with them.

Mr. Buirkle, my philosophy teacher, led me to see that I learned from a subject what the questions I asked allowed me to learn; and that, to learn variously, I should ask various questions. Professor Buirkle was also responsible for some of the thought I put into developing my alternative curriculum.

I remember sitting in the back of his classroom and, along with most of my classmates, trying to take notes on what he and a few of the students were saying about how you knew that you actually knew something. Buirkle said "Whoa," breaking off the conversation. Like a searchlight, he scanned the room, lingering on each of the furious scribblers. "Stop the notetaking. Join the conversation. If you're really involved in it, you'll remember it. When you have your first break, sit and write down what you remember of the conversation. What you capture will be more coherent than the notes you're feverishly scribbling, and it will take up a hell of a lot less space. Finally, when you review for the test, you'll remember it and you may even understand it."

I took his advice, went to South College, and before joining the gang at a table, took my coffee to a solitary spot and wrote up a summary of the class. It took about ten minutes. The Buirkle system worked for Buirkle and most of my English courses. Forget about chemistry. Oh, well, there are some courses the individual just ought to avoid. From Mr. Bloodgood, my economics teacher, I learned how to think about the forces competing for limited resources, and how human beings might behave to create a satisfactory distribution of necessities without blowing everything to smithereens. Bill Bloodgood had a habit of explaining—"boiling it down," he called it, then saying, "That's the way it works, *cateris parabus.*"

I thought I knew what the phrase meant, but I checked it out in John Schmidt's Latin dictionary. (Schmidt, who unofficially moved in with me when Sherwood Powers moved out, was allowed to take Latin because it was new to him. I often helped him with his translations. The stuff was definitely more interesting than the stupid anecdotes that poisoned Spanish for me.) Yes, *cateris parabus*, or "holding other things constant," was the idea; but how the hell would you do that if human beings were part of the "other things?" I asked Bloodgood the question. He laughed and said even dictators failed at that and he, a slippery Keynesian, was no dictator. Then he said maybe the best you could do was to make a theory that floated. I told him I thought I'd major in English instead.

The course that saved my bacon freshman year was the two-semester English sequence requiring reading and writing in a variety of forms. It was taught by Alan McGill. We used a number of books, but the most important one for me was *A Rhetoric Casebook* by Francis Xavier Connolly. Learning how to read the various forms and to use them in organizing my own thinking opened up many possibilities for discovery.

In addition, Alan McGill made me aware of the need to improve my style or, should I say, styles? He cured me of a high school habit of weighing down my sentences with

Latinate vocabulary—it still creeps in once in a while—taught me to be concrete, and encouraged me to master the grammatical rhythms of the language. Why he didn't stay at Dickinson I do not know, but of this I am certain: when he left, the college lost a first-rate teacher.

In my sophomore year, I took the English lit survey with Bert Davis, the best teacher I had had at that point and as good as any I've had since. Bert Davis was a Socratic teacher, leading his students through canonical texts of literature by asking questions that fostered complexity of thought and feeling. It was his romantic poetry course that made me, for a moment, an A student.

Why he didn't remain at Dickinson, I do know. In 1955, the college hired an economist named Raymond LaVallee, who was then investigated by the House Committee on Un-American Activities. In March 1956, President Edel suspended LaVallee. Bert Davis was president of the Dickinson chapter of AAUP. The central purpose of the organization was to defend academic freedom, which meant locking horns with bullheaded administrators and trustees.

By doing his job for a man who had been unfairly suspended, Bert Davis suffered from the anti-communist fervor of President Edel and quite a few of the well-heeled trustees. Because Professor Davis acted responsibly, as his colleagues had elected him to do, he was told that his contract would not be renewed. Though that decision was set aside after widespread student and faculty discontent and Professor Davis did remain at Dickinson the following year, in June of 1957 he left the college to join the staff of AAUP in Washington, DC. He would later become general secretary of the organization. I know that the post was an important one for all who cared about the health and happiness of college teachers, but Bert Davis's being out of teaching was a loss as well, maybe a greater one. Fortunately, I later heard, he eventually got back where he belonged, teaching in a university.

Frank Warlow was the other fine teacher I studied with at Dickinson. He taught the few courses in modern literature offered at the college. His forte was making difficult poetry clear by magnificent readings. To him I owe my introduction to the poetry of W. B. Yeats, the subject, later on, of my master's thesis at Lehigh University. Professor Warlow did remain at Dickinson, and as well as teaching effectively he took up some of the work Bert Davis had done for the AAUP. I had the great fortune of visiting with Professor Warlow at Dickinson's alumni weekends and thanking him for encouraging me to go to graduate school and to become an active member of the AAUP.

Because of these teachers and a number of other advisors, I managed to stay at Dickinson, to complete the requirements, and to give my time to activities that really mattered to me—fraternity life, running a business, singing in the glee club, writing music and lyrics for the Follies and performing in three productions, and spending hours in ongoing debate and in exuberant frolicking with fellow Dickinsonians who, like myself, had discovered the joys of the alternative curriculum.

CHAPTER FOUR

"Clunk-Ta-Tunk": Life at 402 West High Street

There are places in our lives that will always be with us, no matter how far we roam in the accidents and urgencies of life. One of the ones that still occurs in my dreams is the Beta Theta Pi fraternity house at the corner of Moreland and High Streets in Carlisle, Pennsylvania. At least from 1953 through 1957, my time at Dickinson, it still stood there. During most of my days at the college, it was there I ate, slept, read, wrote, sang, danced, drank, and even, believe it or not, studied. The old house is not there anymore, but I could reconstruct it from the *clunk-ta-tunk* of the knocker on its front door that spoke like a Walmart greeter to anyone who entered to the far reaches of its interior.

I can still visualize the spaces of the house. The basement closet, full of paint cans, a tub for cooling a beer keg, several taps, and anything broken that Peppy Knoblauch said he could repair but never got around to. The second floor closet where the files of old tests and term papers were kept, along with signs for glee club concerts, my disabled trombone (Jay Hartman had hidden the mouthpiece), and remnants of old homecoming displays, including a fake historical marker that I made sure my father never discovered. The furnace room, where a worm fed coal into the furnace except when a dog bone jammed the works and the house filled up with noxious vapors. The sacred chapter room in the basement which those who were allowed to enter will have to remember on their own. The double living room where we held the Eye of Wooglin and entertained the ladies. The dining room where Brother Hyman's famous emblem shone down from the far wall. The kitchen where Marion Byers held court. The second basement where canned food and the White Hats' beer were stored and Ted Auman shot rats with a .22.

Up, up and away again to the second floor, to the realm of the brothers' rooms, the two heads, and up even further to the sleeping dorm, one large room filled with beds, its windows nailed open to air the place out and to allow snowflakes to flutter in and land on unprotected toes and heads.

I hardly ever slept in that dorm, having discovered early on—when I was still officially a resident of Conway Hall—the wonderfulness of the couches in the living room at 402.

Semester after semester, I'd move my clothes and other clutter from one room to another, in preparation for which

I painted at least three of those rooms. Some people establish their connection to the world by polishing cars or mowing lawns; I painted rooms, learning enough from the Beta house walls to paint my own house, inside and out, at 508 East Beau Street in Washington, Pennsylvania. In the alternative curriculum, house painting was a credit course.

Another credit came my way through the Beta sandwich business. As a freshman, from time to time, I was hired to sit in a cubbyhole on the first floor of Conway Hall in the space where the sandwich man kept his milk cooler and other supplies. From nine to eleven on evenings when freshmen were supposed to be in the dorm by nine, it was where they could drag their hunger for milk and sandwiches, chips, and pretzels. While Ross Brown and/or John Winand drove around to the women's dorms and the fraternities, I would sit in the cubbyhole, strain my eyes with the history book and wait on customers. I got paid two bucks for an evening's work, and I could eat one sandwich and drink one milk free of charge. I've never been much of a milk drinker, and when I started running track, I cut out the cow entirely because milk thickened my saliva and complicated breathing. Thereafter, I stuck with water; and I sold my carton of milk to someone else and pocketed the coins.

In my sophomore year, Ross Brown retired from the sandwich business; John Winand inherited it; and I became the steady gnome in the cubbyhole, selling sandwiches to the ravenous wolves of Conway, a now-extinct species, gone the way of freshman dinks and signs and a lot of other idiocies. While I sat there, John would drive across Carlisle to Metzger Hall and Gibbs House, the Ellis Islands for freshman women. I know, I know—first-year women, the old language having gone the way of dinks and signs; but that's what we called the ladies locked up in Metzger and Gibbs in the dear old days almost beyond recall. After feeding the females and the fraternities, John would return to Conway and we'd load up his car and finish off the night at Drayer Hall and the law school. Drayer, the main dorm for sophomore, junior, and senior women, was a lucrative stop. The women still had a curfew of 10:15 p.m. Sundays through Thursdays. By the time we got there, it was usually closer to eleven, and our sandwiches were in demand. Selling stuff in Drayer was an enlightening experience, better than the Sears catalog for an introduction to ladies' nightwear and a startling insight into the use of soda cans to encourage a headful of curls!

Our final stop was the law school. The guys, being adults, didn't have hours. Yes, I said guys: if there were any gals, they didn't buy sandwiches. Anyhow, for most of the year, sales in the law school were slow. John sometimes wondered if going there was worth the time. Still, we did show up because on some evenings (payday for those riding the GI Bill?), there would be a mammoth poker game in one of the lounges. We never sold any milk to the players; they had their own beverages—beer and varieties of liquor—but they would holler for sandwiches. I remember John saying on one occasion, "Bill, if you want a sandwich, you'd better take it now; this starving gang is going to buy everything we have left." He was right. We left the law school with a very light load and pockets full of cash. "If we could sell beer," John proclaimed, "we'd be billionaires!" Alternative curriculum credits for what sells and when.

There was one other time, later in the year, when the law school was a gold mine. Near the end of the spring semester, the first-year law students were studying for the one—the one and only—exam in a course that had run all year long. I don't know what it was called, but it kept them in their rooms; no quickie runs for beer to the Jimmie, the Molly, or Frychlands, just stay glued to a chair and memorize, memorize, memorize.

By the time John and I arrived that night, you could hear the empty stomachs rumbling throughout the dorm. Knowing in advance that the hungry mob awaited, John had ordered a load of extra sandwiches. We even figured to sell some milk. It was, indeed, a gold mine. Alternative curriculum points big time!

Not only did we cash in, but I, at least, learned something that would help me plan my future. My mother had always favored law school as a proper destination for me, and I had actually toyed with the idea. But all that memorization, good grief; it gave me the fantods! Then, one evening just as we entered the dorm, a first-year guy came screaming from his room. I thought he must really be starving: we were a tad late. But it wasn't our sandwiches he was storming. He blew right past us, careened down the hallway and, at its end, tried to climb the wall. He would have made it, too, except the force of his assault drove his head into the plaster and knocked him backward on his butt. He lay there still as a stone.

The other first-years came from their rooms to check out the source of the commotion, some of them bitching about the violation of quiet hours. The flattened body in the hallway shut them down fast. One of the older guys who'd been a corpsman in Korea pushed his way through the mob, knelt by the fallen comrade, and shouted, "Get me some cold towels!" He checked the casualty, and when the towels arrived, he placed them on the guy's badly bruised forehead. "Someone call an ambulance." Someone did.

By the time it arrived, the downed man had regained consciousness and was moaning. They carted him off to the Carlisle Hospital. The other first-years weren't in a hurry to get back to the books and the three-by-five cards. John and I sold all our sandwiches, and I decided not to bother with law school. Alternative curriculum credit: know what to stay the hell away from.

When John dumped me off at the Beta house after our evenings selling sandwiches, it was usually midnight or later.

Some of the guys would still be up, playing bridge or poker or sitting around telling lies about their amatory successes. I sat and watched the game or listened to the fabrications. I didn't have anything to add, and I promised myself that if I ever did, I wouldn't. Sometimes you can learn what not to do by listening to other jerks.

Out of one of those bull-sessions came my reentry to the world of dangerous games. One of the brothers, an older guy fond of ridiculing me, challenged my silence: "Hey, Eavesdropper, what do you got to say for yourself? No, wait, you don't even have a girlfriend. That's it! You don't have anything to say because you've got nothing to talk about."

He was correct, so I said, "Nope, not at the moment," hoping that would get him off my case.

"Not back in Harrisburg, either, I bet."

"Nope, none there either. The girl I dated in high school has a college senior to squire her around these days."

"I bet you never had one. Did you ever have a date?"

"Think what you want. I had dates. Quite a few with one girl I liked a lot."

"Why haven't you ever brought her here?"

"I told you; she found an older guy. He had a car. And I was too busy working and running track to start chasing another girl."

"So, Peachy Keen, you just chased other guys around the track?"

"In my senior year I usually led them around the track—even beat Hal Swidler, Harrisburg's best, in the district meet."

"Come on, what about in the summertime? What did you do in the summertime? Only Olympians run track in the summertime."

"I worked a lot, played a lot of softball and basketball, and I did spend time at the track, practicing the discus and the high jump."

"Why would anyone do that instead of chasing girls?"

"The girls I was interested in had already been chased and caught. And I was practicing the discus and the high jump because my track coach had been talking up the decathlon. Bob Mathias had won the gold at Helsinki in 1952. I couldn't beat my black teammates in the 100 and the 220, but I could stay close, even closer in the 440. I could win the 880 and the mile. I was trying to improve in a couple more events. And you're wrong; there are track meets in the summer—even for high school guys."

"Good grief, Peachy Keen; that's the longest speech you've made since you've been at Dickinson. Why didn't you go out for track here?"

"I'm developing new interests. I'm in the glee club now. Next year, I'll try out for the Follies. And I'm selling sandwiches—hope to run the business when John Winand graduates. Maybe I'll even chase a couple of girls. Besides, I did go out for track last year."

"Bullshit! I never saw you run in a meet."

"Because I never did. When the Beta house lunch went to track practice with me and Steckbeck ran me in the 440 against three seniors, I stayed with them, but I left my lunch at the side of the track. Wasn't much chance I was going to change the house lunches, and I couldn't afford to eat elsewhere. So track and I bid each other farewell. Still, I'm thinking about a summer program. I could eat my mother's cooking, which has never made me sick, and work on the discus and the high jump."

"Decathlon? Discus? High Jump? You're bullshitting me."

"Screw you: I'll show you." I'd had enough of him. I stormed up to the sleeping dorm, liberated a mattress—waking up some early-to-bed brothers who grumbled and swore at me—and dragged it thumpingly down to the first floor. I pulled a high-backed easy chair to the end of the mattress and balanced three thick sofa cushions on the top of the chair. "That's well over five feet: jump over it." Jordy Ewell had usually won the high jump at John Harris with jumps of six feet: and he was a specialist. Fosbury had not yet begun to flop. "Go ahead; jump over it. No, second thought, I'll take the pillows off. There, that's under five feet. Jump over it."

"You're the athlete; you jump over it."

"OK. Big-mouth bows out by refusing to jump over less than five feet." I again put the three sofa cushions on the top of the chair back.

"Clunk-ta-tunk!" Tommy Hough and Kenny Hitchner had just entered the scene, most likely having been tippling at the Femina Bar. "What's going on?" Tom Hough asked.

"Peachy Keen thinks he can jump over the chair and three cushions."

"Yeah, and loudmouth won't even try it without the cushions," I countered.

"I got two bucks says he can," said one of the poker players hanging out waiting for a game. That stimulated a flurry of betting.

"OK. OK. I have to clear the top cushion and not knock it off."

"Yeah, and you get three attempts to do it."

"Thanks, but I doubt I'll need them."

I plotted out a runway up to the chair, took off my shoes, made a slow-motion practice run at the back of the chair, returned to the head of the run, surged forward, leapt, and cleared the chair and three cushions with room to spare. "Stuff that where the sun don't shine," I said, aiming the words at the now-silenced face of my tormentor. Those who had bet on me were approaching loudmouth and two others of little faith. Loudmouth, grumbling, paid up and headed up the stairs.

On that evening of gym credit in the alternative curriculum and the promise of free beers from the guys who'd profited from my leaping ability, Tom Hough, Kenny Hitchner, and I decided to continue the jumping. We founded the One to Three A.M. Tumbling Club of Beta Theta Pi. After that, we performed most weeknights and even sometimes at parties, aided by an infusion of the electric soup. People came and went as graduation and enlistment exercised their pull on our numbers; but there were always new pledges to join the game. I don't know how long our organization lasted, but it was still going when I graduated in 1957, when, among others, my little brother, Hank Menin, was jumping over cushions and chairs.

Hitchner hadn't been in Dickinson when I first arrived. He was spending a semester at Wilkes College, bolstering his average to return and have another go at Dickinson. He came back in January of 1954, adding one more piano player to the corps as well as a damn fine bass voice. We started to sing together at the house and in the glee club, and, later on, collaborated putting words to music for the Follies, a yearly event in the alternative curriculum started up in 1949. I don't know who actually gets credit for that; but, according to Hitchner, in 1950 and for several years after, the soul of the Follies was Ham Neely, a law student who'd majored in extracurricular music-making at Princeton. But I've got to believe that, in the early years, Ken Hitchner and other Dickinsonians with time on their hands and songs in their hearts were important attendant spirits.

In the fall of 1954, Neely had left; but Hitchner and a considerable cast of others who'd been part of *The Sphinx*

Winks and subsequent Follies productions were still around and raring to go. The following spring's show would be *Bachelors' Bend,* written by Eleanor Pocious and Pete Miller.

Hitchner got a copy of the script. Then he lured me out of an infrequent study session to read it. I finished it that night. The next morning, while he and I were waiting tables at breakfast, he gave me my assignment. "We need songs. You and I are going to write some after you come back from selling sandwiches—no tumbling until we're done with it." Alternative curriculum credits were having a ball. Over the next month and a half, we spent all our spare time (and a lot we stole from other studies) singing, rhyming, and revising. I fed him lyrics. He suited them up with music. Then we argued, wrote, and rewrote until we got them more or less right.

Out of the five or six songs we actually put together, we submitted three to the director, Cody Brookes. He and his committee chose two of them, "A Guest in the West" and "I Could Fall in Love So Easily." Hitchner wrote another, entitled simply "Blues Number." What Dick Swenson had to do with it as the program says he did, I don't know: but when Hitchner played it for me, I tinkered with it. Hey, anything to help!

Later that fall, word got around that the GI Bill was about to end. Guys who hoped to use it had better get signed up for service in a hurry. Kenny, who was already in his fifth year of college and needed at least two more to graduate, decided to leave school at the end of the semester and collect some gelt to pay for his extended education. The alternative curriculum has always been underfunded.

In the second semester, there wasn't much tumbling and the pianos sat as silent as tombs. For two weeks in January and most of February, I actually studied and went to class, and, as usual, sold sandwiches. It's a good thing I did study a bit before it was time to try out for the Follies. When Hitchner had left, he'd encouraged me to try out. "Go for the chorus or a small speaking part," he advised. That sounded good to me. I thought they could use my voice in the chorus. So I went down to the practice room in Denny, sang a few songs, hoofed through a grapevine, and projected some lines at the boys and girls in the back row.

On the day when the names of those selected for the cast were to be posted on the bulletin board by South College, I walked over that way. A couple of coeds coming back from South toward Drayer smiled and congratulated me. I guessed I'd made the chorus. There was a crowd at the bulletin board. One of the guys spotted me and said, "Hey, there, Whitie." Another said, "Here comes the star!" Whitie? The star? What the hell was going on? I wormed my way in to read the list. Yep, there was my name—not in the chorus but in the role of Whitie, the romantic lead. I was floored. Whitie? I'd read the script. Whitie had a lot of lines. I thought I'd be singing and dancing and maybe uttering one or two lines; but all of that—how would I ever get it memorized?

I retreated to South for a cup of coffee. At the snack bar, I ran into Margot Patrick. As a dancer, she'd had something to do with casting. I asked her why I'd been cast as the lead, reminding her that I'd been aiming for the chorus, and that, basically, I was a singer. Maybe the committee wasn't impressed with my dancing, which, admittedly, was less than smooth. All she said was, "Bill, you'll be fine." A fraternity brother later speculated that I'd been chosen because, as a blushing blonde lad, I looked the part. I considered dyeing my hair.

I'm not an actor. But after my athletic failures, I was beginning to feel like a quitter. So I accepted the part. And I got through it; but I doubt that I was fine. The high point of my performance occurred when Margot, masquerading as an Indian squaw, snuck up and clobbered me on the head; I did a fine job of falling down. Then, later on, when I sang my solo, no one booed; I guess that's something. Even the alternative curriculum can throw curveballs. Watch your head!

The next year, the Follies staged *Jamaican Jaunt*, a calypso-highlighted holiday. Dutch Skeel and Doug Wert, both Betas and both better choices for a lead role than I'd been, did a great job as a kind of Crosby and Hope type duo. I concentrated on writing lyrics and practicing my dance steps, vowing that no director would again cast me in a big role.

The chorus was good enough. I'd try to improve my dancing and not trip over my own feet. One or two lines? Yeah, maybe.

CHAPTER FIVE

Sandwiches and Milk: The Production Number

In his junior year, John Winand got married, gave up the sandwich business, and began working at an accounting firm in Carlisle. I took over the sandwich business a year early and managed it until I graduated. My associate was Bill Corey, a Beta brother a year behind me. Like me, Bill was trying to get through Dickinson without bankrupting his parents. I had come back to Carlisle in the fall without the help of my parents. Was I growing up? I'd loaded my stuff in the '46 Chevy I'd inherited from Pappy when he moved up to a Pontiac. Things were looking up for him. The federal government was partnering with states to clean up our rivers by constructing more sophisticated sewage disposal plants for small towns along their banks. The program targeted the Susquehanna, and Pappy's employer, Gannett, Fleming, won some of the contracts.

For the sandwich business I did all the ordering, shopping around Carlisle for the best deals on ham and cheese, going to wholesalers for large cans of chicken and tuna, and contracting with a local poultry farmer for good eggs at a decent price. Believe me, eggs differ. You want to buy a variety that has flavor but not so much that after three weeks in the cool cellar it becomes too strong. You don't want the customers smelling the egg salad before you get to the dorm. John had taught me the ropes, and I tried to improve their pull. I also hired fraternity brothers to make the sandwiches. Bood Wright, Jay Hartman, Bob Singdahlsen, and Bob Armacost worked for me at one time or another. And the Beta cook, Marion Byers, kept me informed about sales.

Bill Corey and I sold the sandwiches: peanut butter and jelly (twenty cents); ham and cheese on white or rye; egg salad, tuna salad, and chicken salad on white (twenty-five cents); and for Jeannie Carlson, one of my very favorite ladies, a tuna on rye and a pickle (thirty cents). Jeannie was a girl I would have chased, always liked those Swedes! But an older Beta, Lenny Spangler, had returned from the navy and beat me to her.

We also sold some accoutrements to sandwiches and milk—pretzels, potato chips, and cheese crackers. As a devoted Utz man, I would have stocked their stuff, but George Bobolitz, the business manager who oversaw all the student businesses, said I had to stick with Snyders because Gary

Sterner, a student at Dickinson, was somehow related to the family. Sorry, Utz, you do what you have to do.

It was through the sandwich business that I had my first run-in with the Carlisle police. One evening I arrived at Metzger with my cartons of sandwiches and milk and was granted admission to the ground level by the student proctor in charge. I was positioning my wares on a table at the end of a long hallway and was just about to yodel, "Sandwiches and milk," when Mrs. Grubb appeared. Mrs. Grubb seemed to me very severe and unsmiling. Maybe I was the victim of stereotypical thinking and just couldn't see her gentler qualities. Maybe she had gentler qualities, but I never got to experience them. Possibly it was just the nature of her job. I don't know. But I knew I had to put a good face on it and stay on her better side, if I could figure out where that was. I'd certainly try. After all, I'd had plenty of experience dealing with several judgmental women at 2033 Whitehall Street.

On that evening, Mrs. Grubb commandeered me, ordering me to climb up the fire escape to see if there was a Peeping Tom lurking there. I left my merchandise sitting on the table in the dorm's basement and walked back up the hallway and outside to do as she had asked. I found no one. But as I made my way back down, the Carlisle police found me and were about to haul me into the station as the Peeping Tom. I protested that Mrs. Grubb had ordered me to go up the fire escape and do a check. The cop looked at me askance.

"Hey, officer," I said, "it's always a good idea to stay on the right side of that old lady," the old lady who, along with the student proctor, had disappeared.

Apparently, the cop had been down Mrs. Grubb's street before, because he almost choked trying to suppress laughter. I sensed an easing of his suspicions. Standing by the door to the basement which, fortunately, had a window in it, I pointed down the hallway at my stuff still sitting on the table at the end: "Look, there's my sandwiches; just ring the bell until the proctor comes, and she'll back me up. Please, check it out. I'll tell you right now what all's in that box."

The cop rang the bell. The proctor who'd let me in before reappeared and opened the door. The cop and I entered and we all walked down the hallway to the table. It seemed like a longer walk this time. My knees were shaking. The cop inspected my wares. "Do you know him?" the cop asked the proctor.

"Oh, yes, officer, he's the Beta Sandwich Man," she said.

"And he's allowed to be in here?"

"Oh, yes, sir; we look forward to his arrival with sandwiches and milk."

"OK," the cop said. He turned and began to walk back out.

I called after him, "Officer, would you like a sandwich, on the house?"

He looked back over his shoulder, said "No thanks," and left.

A line of hungry coeds was beginning to form. "C'mon, Mr. Beta man, we're starving!" one of them complained.

"Just a second, please." Before selling anything, I asked the proctor to choose whatever she liked, on the house. She chose a chicken salad sandwich and a small chocolate milk. I handed her a bag of chips as well. It was almost like a date.

The excitement of the evening and the long wait had produced impressive appetites in the Metzger girls. The line was long. By the time I'd waited on all of them, there wasn't much left for the Gibbs House girls across the street; but I got by because, though they, too, had waited longer than usual, they didn't appear to be starving. Driving back to Conway to pick up Bill Corey, I wondered what had become of Mrs. Grubb after she'd sent me up the fire escape. She'd completely disappeared. The more I picked at that scab, the more irritated I became. Had she set me up? Had she wanted me to visit the Carlisle jail, maybe even spend the night there?

The following summer I spent two months at Dickinson's summer school trying to raise my average by taking only two courses at a time. It worked. I got a flock of B's. Basically, it was a dull summer—not much to do except go to class and study. Once in a while a couple of us would pile into a car and go off to a drive-in movie at the Silver Springs or down the road in Newville or maybe have a few beers at Fryckland's or just take a walk on the flat streets of Carlisle, so easy to stroll on without breaking a sweat. One evening Creighton Reed, Bill Corey, and I were ambling along out near the Walnut Bottom Tavern, Fryckland's new name after a change in management. We'd just crossed the street when Reed impulsively grabbed the road sign pole and began to shinny up. He hung on to the signs and twisted until he'd shifted them sufficiently to misidentify the streets at the intersection. "Hey, man, why the hell'd you do that?" I asked, having been victimized by shifted signs in unfamiliar places in my own past wanderings.

If he had a reason, he didn't say. Maybe he was tired of giving reasons. Summer school classes might have three or four students instead of the usual fifteen to twenty. You couldn't escape professors' questions and the demand for reasons, reasons, and more reasons. Small classes aren't always an advantage.

We hadn't walked more than half a block beyond the scene of the crime when the Carlisle police arrived and detained us. Reed had been spotted by a citizen with a telephone. We were escorted to the police station and lectured by the officer manning the desk. "Don't you know there's a hospital nearby? That kind of act could complicate an emergency."

I took his point, but I didn't appreciate his directing the scolding rhetoric at me. Apparently, he'd decided I was the ringleader. But I kept my mouth shut. We all did. And at least one of us looked as if he'd been whipped. Fortunately, a tongue-lashing was all we were in for. Who knows? Maybe the jail was full.

CHAPTER SIX

Getting Out of the House: Singers, Dancers, and Roisterers

As important as the fraternity was to me—and I believe that many of the lasting connections I made at Dickinson emanated from Beta Theta Pi—I was never exclusively tied to the house. Sure, I was called the Beta Sandwich Man; and I appreciated the fact that people recognized who I was and where I belonged; but unlike some of my fellow Betas for whom the fraternity was the primary, maybe the only identification, I had, almost from the beginning, connections beyond the Halls of Wooglin, the secular spirit land of Beta Theta Pi. As time went on, certainly from the beginning of my junior year, I developed connections outside the house.

One of my good friends from freshman year in Conway Hall, Dick Seeburger, was a force not only in his own fraternity, Phi Delta Theta, but widely about the campus. Not that I could ever be as strong a student as he, but I hoped that, as far as activities were concerned, I had a similar campus involvement.

Actually, for encouraging me against becoming a fraternity troglodyte, I owe John Winand, my first contact with Beta and my boss in the sandwich business. On a ride back to Carlisle after Thanksgiving vacation freshman year, he counseled me not to get stuck in a rut. As I've said, John was older, a veteran, and he constantly had jobs that gave him some distance from 402 West High Street. Even when he was on campus, he occupied himself in organizations that reached beyond the fraternity—the glee club, student government, and, of course, the sandwich business. "Some of our more zealous fraternity brothers shit pink and blue," he told me, and broke into his cackle of a laugh. (Pink and blue were our frat-lodge colors.) I'd tried to follow his lead, not only in joining a number of campus-wide activities, but also in seeking out guys I'd met, to chat with over coffee in South College, for example.

I often met up with Mike Shapell, Rod Harvey, and Dick Seeburger, all members of the glee club, at the Jimmie or the Molly or Fryckland's—the well-known watering holes of Carlisle back then. Between classes at South College we'd often get together—and on the road trips to give concerts for alumni groups and, once, to make a record in New York City. We drank and sang together in local bars after the concerts. At a down-and-under joint in Greenwich Village, following our recording date, we sang again the whole concert. After the first round of beer and the first song, we didn't have to buy another drink. The other customers kept pitchers coming our way. By New York standards, the locals were getting a bargain evening of entertainment. From the way we talked, argued, planned, and joked around with one another you might have thought we were all members of the same house as, in a sense, we were, the house of Gotta Singa Song.

In recent years—for more than twenty now—the members of the glee club have done a reunion in Carlisle the second weekend of June. Fifteen years ago, we invited the Octels, a group formed long after we'd all graduated, to join us. They're now the majority. But I still get to fill out a chord with Bud Gaynor, Chuck Ferrone, and Ken Hitchner. Sad to say, Bill Haupt, who was the heart and soul of the glee club after Frank Oglesby graduated, is now singing with the angels—check that, he's leading them in song.

For most of my senior year I roomed with Richard Nelson Hyman, a junior from Baltimore and a very talented painter, who actually stuck to his vision and became a successful artist in Ellicott City. He was, I thought, a creative genius. Yeah, I know, some of the brothers thought he was just a pain in the ass; but they should have been directed to the drugstore for some Preparation H. In his spare time, Brother Hyman took to decorating the house. On the back wall of the dining room, he painted the Beta seal, Wooglin seated on

a shield; and in the bathrooms he inscribed terrifying creatures of myth meant to irritate members of the Pink and Blue
Inquisition and perhaps to shock any coed who slipped away
from a room party or Sunday's gin and juice to the designated "ladies' room" for a quiet pee. Credit in the alternative
curriculum? Sure, but in what subject—art or psychology?

Maybe I shouldn't say I roomed with Richard, because I
often found the door to "our" room locked. Could he have
been studying? He did take to that activity more readily than
I. But it's also possible that he was playing house. Was that a
part of the alternative curriculum, too? I must have missed
it. Studying or entertaining a lady wasn't the only reason for
the locked door, however. Though he ended up an art and
English type, Richard had started out as a premed. The shift
in direction didn't quite cure him of his love of chemistry—
or was it alchemy? He did occasionally mutter what sounded like spells. (One I remember was something about lonely
men in shirt sleeves.) Was he on a search for the philoso-
pher's stone? If he found it, he never said. But what he did
manage to concoct with a primitive still made up of a flask,
corks, and glass tubes he'd liberated from the Chemistry
Department was a throat-burning concoction. He enjoined
me to sample it. The clear liquid looked like gin, so I had a
go at it. The product burned like a fireball going down, but
fortunately there wasn't enough of it to do sustained damage
to the guinea pig.

Richard had better luck with his concoctions when he relied on spirits that were actually for sale in the state store. One of these he called a Charlie Brown, in honor of his favorite cartoon character. I don't recall everything that went into it—Cherry Herring, I think, and some other potent juice. I've since run into versions of this beverage called Callugaberry Punch, a sickeningly sweet drink that fraternity lads at another school mixed up in a huge plastic trash bin. (Stay away from it. In fact, stay away from any drinks you don't open or pour for yourself or are poured for you by someone you unflinchingly trust. Even followers of the alternative curriculum need to remain sentient.) Richard's Charlie Browns were mild in comparison, largely because he didn't have the gelt to fill up a trash container with booze. Relative poverty can be a blessing. But maybe he was just being frugal.

The summer before Richard and I began to room together, he'd found enough money to take a trip to Europe and gaze upon the paintings in most of its famous galleries. On this jaunt, he'd hooked up with a Dickinson classmate, Robertson Taylor. Robertson belonged to the Phi Kap fraternity, but he was definitely a free soul. Practically everyone knew who Robertson was, because in his freshman year he'd led a rowdy bunch by chanting in his booming bass voice, "Down with the Black Hats." The Black Hats were the junior bigwigs in charge of pestering freshmen during orientation.

What earthly good they did I couldn't fathom. Even stupid traditions have their advocates. Apparently Robertson's followers thought so too.

In the fall following Richard's summer abroad, he often regaled me with stories about Robertson. The big guy wasn't much for art museums, Hyman said; but he did like the nightlife, drinking the various fermented fluids of Holland, Belgium, and France and, in Pigalle, chatting up the dancers and other professional ladies and buying everyone at the bar a round. By the time I finally met Robertson, he was living in an apartment conveniently near the Femina Bar and that late-night eatery, the Hamilton Restaurant. No one ever called it that. It was and is to this day the H. A. Milton, owned originally, myth has it, by the poet John's younger brother. Robertson's place was a famous party pad visited frequently by guys and gals who were stepping beyond the fraternities and sororities. Hyman was already a regular there, as well as Tony Tsigunus, whose relative may have owned the H. A. Milton; and Jules Takacs, a brave Hungarian who had escaped the communists, come to America, found his way to Dickinson, and been taken in by the Betas, but was led elsewhere by Robertson, who became his lifelong friend, dutifully visiting him at his home in eastern Pennsylvania when Jules was dying of cancer. Robertson Taylor stuck with his friends. I would soon be counted as one of them.

I first met the big bass horn that was Robertson Blaylock Taylor at Fryckland's (was it spelled with an i or a y? I should know, being an English teacher). On that evening, I was enjoying beers and the free pretzels with Heber Harper, Ray Stone, and several Betas when Robertson came bounding into the place followed by Hyman, who was almost obscured by the room-filling bulk of his friend.

"Where is the famous sandwich man Richard has been telling me about?"

Heber Harper ratcheted forth his hacking laugh, "Ack, ack, ack!" He sounded like an unoiled metal gate swinging in a windstorm.

"I don't know about the famous part, but I am the Beta Sandwich Man."

"Then you must be William Parker Keen," he said, turning to Hyman for verification: "Richard, is this not the famous sandwich man, William Parker Keen?"

"Yes, Robertson Blaylock, that is he. I call him W. Parker Keen, though he prefers Will or Wump."

True, since grade school where the teachers turned Wil-li-am into a whip of reprimand, I had preferred Bill; the college names Will or Wump were OK too. Robertson and Hyman had been abroad; the two of them had taken to a lordly style of address.

"My good man, clearly you are the famous sandwich man who can march into Drayer Hall and survey the pulchritude contained therein. Mr. Keen, I suggest you need a partner, and I, the product of a long line of mercantile masterminds, volunteer my services."

"Thanks, but I have a partner." I pointed out Bill Corey, who sat across the table from me.

"Hmm, yes, Mr. Corey. We entered this college together as freshmen. Did you chant 'Down with the Black Hats,' Mr. Corey?"

"I might have whispered it," Corey replied.

"Good answer," I said.

"Did you think I was addressing you, Mr. Keen, the famous sandwich man?"

"No, but I thought every mainline performer needs a backup group."

"Really, why so?"

"Don't you listen to popular music? Bing Crosby, backed up by the Andrews sisters or what's-his-face with the Norman Luboff Choir, or almost any rock-and-roller for that matter?"

"Mr. Crosby is respectable, particularly together with Mr. Armstrong. But, frankly, between you and I, rock and roll is a passing fancy. I'd much rather hear—" he paused, took a deep breath, and belted out, "Hail, Britannia, Britannia rules the waves!"

"I listen to that, too," I said to the singer; "I try to have catholic tastes."

"Rather, I myself no longer attend church services; but I used to be a Presbyterian."

"Neither do I. I'm supposed to be a Quaker; but there's no meeting in Carlisle."

"Ack, ack, ack," Heber Harper hacked in, "Er, that's right, er, but there's one in Harrisburg." I don't know whether Heber ever officially joined a meeting. He'd started off as a Methodist, but he'd gone to college at Haverford; and he acted like a Quaker, doing a lot of little good works that people seldom gave him credit for.

Robertson and Richard joined us. Most of us were drinking beer. Robertson announced that he'd prefer a Gibson or some scotch: but at Fryckland's you could get either beer or beer, a fact that endeared the place to me because a date couldn't order one of those expensive glo-winky drinks served in a martini glass and sporting a little umbrella for a swizzle stick. Even the famous sandwich man had to husband his nickels and dimes.

So the big guy drank beer—actually a six-pack's worth in an hour's time—and he ate most of the pretzels. By the end of the evening, we were singing, Robertson doing the bass part on "Old Man River," going right down there, in Paul Robeson style, and landing solidly on the low note in "we land in ja-il" and following that with a solo of "My Father Killed a Kangeroo." He should have been in the glee club.

After that evening Robertson became a regular at the Wednesday afternoon parties that Hyman and I hosted at the Beta house. Guys who were in the ROTC had to put on their uniforms and attend drill on Wednesday, as I had done in my first two years. Hyman, who'd started out as a pre-med, thought that would keep him out of the draft, so he'd foregone the experience of ROTC and Wednesday afternoon drill. Like me, Robertson had opted out after two years. Our alternative curriculum substitution for drill was hoisting a glass at the Beta house and dancing with as many coeds as we could lure away from other studies. It was a growing number.

Ray Stone, a popular poli-sci professor and quite an avid tippler at Fryckland's, had an apartment near Metzger where he hosted discussion groups on Wednesday nights to argue about national events and drink beer. He'd invite heavy-hitting students and other youngish faculty members who, unlike most of Dickinson's students, might have been Democrats, or at least leaning that way. Robertson and Hyman hadn't registered to vote because neither was twenty-one. I had just become legal but had not yet voted.

Eisenhower was president. My parents, registered Republicans who'd voted for Ike, both disliked Tricky Dicky. It pained my mother to say so, because Nixon was a Quaker. My father didn't like him and it didn't pain him to say so. Their attitudes toward the man made it easier for me to stay open about my politics and not, just by habit, go the

Republican way, as had all Parker and Keen flesh before me. I didn't have strong feelings about any of the candidates; but one thing bothered me: every time Ike was photographed on a golf course, he was surrounded by other white golfers. The only black man making his way into the picture was a caddy toting someone's bags.

I'd mentioned my dissatisfaction at Fryckland's one night when Robertson, Ray Stone, and Heber Harper were there. Robertson, who'd grown up in a Democratic family, had been holding forth about his hero, Harry Truman. I hadn't given much thought to Truman except that dropping the *two* bombs had upset both me and my mother. Heber seemed to agree with me. I'm not sure about Stone. But I think it was my beginning to gnaw at politics and Robertson's championing of Truman that got us invited to the next discussion session at Stone's apartment. Neither of us was in poli-sci—just two flaky English majors—and neither of us was on the fast track to Phi Beta Kappa or graduate school.

It didn't take me long to suspect that we'd been invited because Ray Stone was at least as interested in beer as in world affairs. Robertson was a booming presence, and I tried to slip in something relevant now and then. The other students present were all heavy hitters. I could see why Ray Stone approved of them. He'd no doubt write recommendations for them to work for advanced degrees at Princeton or Syracuse.

The scholars left at about nine thirty, but Robertson and I stayed on for another round. When the beer was gone and we were about to leave, I visited the head. I found one of the other young professors asleep in the tub where he was taking a nap underneath a xylophone. Why? I do not know. I played a few notes, and he began to stir. I freed him from his musical accompaniment and fished him out. Ray Stone would have to drive him back to campus, thus cancelling his intention to continue the discussion at a local bar. Liberal education, that's what we called it.

I have always been a walker. Whether carting newspapers around Allison Hill or hoofing it downtown to a movie or across the Walnut Street Bridge to Island Park for a swim in the Susquehanna or to see the Senators play, my preferred form of locomotion was the shoe leather express. In my eighties now, I still try to walk every day in the relatively flat area near my house or, on bad weather days, on an indoor track where senior citizens share the space with middle schoolers.

At Dickinson, I fell in with a group of Betas who took advantage of the flatness of Carlisle to exercise and, particularly on Sundays, to walk off the effects of Saturday nights. Jay Hartman, Bob Singdahlson, and I were dedicated members. Sometimes, one or another of the pledges would join us. Ted Auman, seeing us heading out for a jaunt, would laugh at our departing backs and settle back down to a leisurely read of the Sunday paper. Ted was not a walker. He'd had more than enough walking around the parade ground at Culver Military Academy to last him a lifetime. He owned an Olds Super 88, and he was determined to use it, even to drive it from the Beta house to the Baird biology building, only two blocks apart. Occasionally, he'd preempt our Sunday afternoon hike by hauling Singdahlson and me and some others to further destinations in his fancy car.

It was easy for Ted to convince Sing to hop in the Olds, because Sing was a car enthusiast who'd come to college intending to become an automotive designer. I think he must have been bitten by an enticement put out nationwide to junior high school students by General Motors. The company encouraged students to design the car of the future and enter their designs in a contest which would win a handful of the hopefuls scholarships to engineering programs. Bobby's struggles in a whomping freshman math course ended that dream, sending him into English and acting, in the latter of which he truly excelled. I didn't fancy walking by myself, so when Ted invited Sing, I'd tag along.

Off we'd zoom to the Gettysburg battlefield, Fuller Lake, or a site near the top of a local mountain known as Wagner's Gap. When the college had gobbled up half our football field by building Morgan Hall in 1955, excursions to green spaces outside Carlisle picked up. Ted's car was the usual bus. If we were going to play nine holes at Camp Shand, we'd use Bob

Armacost's jalopy. Ted Auman didn't play golf. His sports were shooting rifles and driving big cars.

Robertson also had a succession of old cars that had belonged to H. G., his gruff old man. Robertson would inherit a near-wreck that HG wasn't going to put any more money into and run it into the ground in a couple of weeks. Most of the times I rode with him, however, it was on the back of the BMW he'd brought back from Europe after his jaunt with Richard the summer before.

The first time Robertson took me for a ride that fall, he arrived at the Beta house on the machine and bellowed up at our open window, "Richard Nelson Hyman and/or William Parker Keen, the famous sandwich man, come down from that cave and go for a ride! First man down wins the seat!" Richard was somewhere else, painting pictures or chasing a lady, and I had intended to study. There wasn't going to be much of a competition for the seat. I stuck my head out the window and shouted, "Looks like you struck out, Robertson. Hyman's not here, and I'm studying."

"Oh, Keen, don't be such an old stick. It's a beautiful day for a ride through the countryside: and on the way back we can stop at Fryckland's for a beer, or, better still, somewhere that serves real drinks."

"Beer is fine with me."

"Good, you're easy to please, Keen."

"How about the Jimmy, Robertson?"

"Why, may I ask, Keen?"

"It's walking distance back to campus, and if you have a number of those real drinks you prefer, I'm not climbing back on that machine."

"Oh, all right, one of little faith. The James Wilson Hotel it will be. Perhaps I'll make an evening of it, have dinner at the H. A. Milton, put the machine away, and climb the stairs to my flat. You can walk home whenever you please."

Sometimes you just have to negotiate the terms in advance. "I'll be right down," I said, and closed the boring book for Professor Prinz's class, economic geography. The subject wasn't boring. The book certainly was. And getting ready for the test was sheer memory work. Another easy A course I'd get a D in.

Down on High Street, Robertson straddled the machine, commanded me to hurry up, and roared the motor. He pointed to the seat behind him and told me to hold on to the strap. I sat and held on. Robertson did a U and turned onto Moreland. After a couple of jigs and jogs, we were approaching the outskirts of Carlisle. A road with fields on both sides lay ahead of us. Robertson took a right onto another country road and soon we were gunning along a bottom with a good-sized stream running along the road to the left. We stopped. "Off, Keen," Robertson said.

Gladly, I thought to myself. After that short ride, my butt was already paralyzed. "How the hell does anyone ride one of these things all over Europe? We've been going twenty minutes and my ass is already asleep," I complained.

"Padding, Keen, padding," Robertson said. I think I understood why Hyman had left his BMW in Europe.

"Keen, you look crippled; perhaps you should try standing."

"Standing? On what? Are you crazy?"

"Oh, Keen, don't be such an old stick."

Robertson bounded to the side of the creek, bent down, and picked up a flat pebble. "Watch this, Keen: observe the master at work."

He skimmed the pebble along the surface of the water, skipping it four times by my count. "Match that, Keen, if you think you can." I picked up a flat pebble and skipped it four times.

"Not bad, Keen; not bad for a sandwich man."

"I grew up on a river."

"Have another go," Robertson, the pseudo-Brit, intoned.

"Nope, I'll settle for a tie."

"Oh, Keen, you are…"

"Yeah, I know, 'an old stick.'"

We reboarded the bike and soon were flying along a road bounded by farmers' fields. If my reckoning was accurate, and I won't swear that it was, we were going toward the Newville drive-in. Robertson came to a screeching halt. I almost went airborne. "What the hell? Are you trying to kill me?"

"Nonsense, Keen: observe." He gestured toward a herd of somnolent-looking cows in the field we'd nearly crash-landed in. He revved his motor fiercely. Several of the cows looked his way.

"Not enough. Come on, girls." He revved his motor even more fiercely. Several more cows looked his way. One or two of them mooed. "Still pretty feckless, girls." He revved the motor until it not only roared—it actually screamed. All the cows turned toward Robertson, lifted their snouts, and poured forth a chorus of moos.

"Much better, my Dears," Robertson said and recited,

I never saw a purple cow,

I hope I never see one,

But I can tell you anyhow,

I'd rather see than be one.

He followed the verse with his customary encore, "My Father Killed a Kangaroo." The cows seemed to prefer the second number. Robertson looked my way, flashed a little smile, and said, "Every actor needs an audience, Keen: you ought to know that. Tally-ho," Robertson whooped: "Off to the James Wilson for a beverage. I'm buying, Keen."

"Good enough," I said: "the cost of the audition."

CHAPTER SEVEN

Hell Is a Hell of a Place:
This Is the Follies, Here, My Son...

In 1957, Mal Rosenberg, Jerry Epstein, Bob Gleeson, and Dick Seeburger teamed up to write the book for *Shades of Hades,* the production the Follies would put on the following spring after dozens of Dickinsonians had pitched in to round out the performance with music and lyrics, dance numbers, ideas for sets, costumes and props, and schemes to make enough money to get the show on the stage. And, oh, yes, finding the best people on campus to make up the cast. Many of the roles, the singers, and the dancers would be filled through auditions, or so we hoped; but we knew it would be necessary to convince people with talent to try out. Those guys and gals often had multiple talents, and they tended to get tied up in multiple activities. We needed a proper devil and adequate cohorts to undermine the innocence of the goody-two-shoes college, Prudy U.

Margot Patrick was set to be the director, and she and Ann Saunders thought they had the lead dancers lined up. Tryouts, we thought, would bring us more dancers and singers and bit-part players. Margot had her eye on Bud Gaynor for the romantic lead, a suave Mephistopheles sent from Hell to seduce the beautiful but naïve queen of virtue among the coeds of Prudy U. We were still looking for that young lady and were hoping the tryouts would bring forth a winner. The biggest role not assigned was the devil. He needed to be a guy who could fill up the stage with energy and personality. Various energetic and charming men had been approached, but we'd struck out in our attempts to get any one of them to try out.

At a meeting of the officers at South College, where most serious business of the Follies was done, people were expressing their nervousness. As we discussed the reluctance of all the candidates, several of us were growing fearful that we might fail to fill a vital role. Margot Patrick knew how to keep her cool and often could calm down others who weren't so adept at staying focused. I was a chief fretter. "Don't worry, Bill; we'll find someone," she said.

"Well, don't look at me," I said: "maybe Dick Seeburger…"

"Present and accounted for but not available for the part," Dick Seeburger said. I stared into my coffee cup, hoping maybe to draw forth from the dregs a spirit with a suggestion. For a couple of minutes no one spoke. Margot finally ended our silent séance.

"How about Robertson Taylor?" she asked.

"By damn, you're right, Margot! Why didn't I think of Robertson?" Maybe because Robertson wasn't exactly the volunteering type, unless it was to have a party. Still, I thought, Robertson would be wonderful in the part. He wouldn't have to act at all. He *was* the devil!

"Do you think he would do it, Bill?"

"Yes, Margot, I think he could be convinced to take the part. You know, Robertson is always looking for an audience. I think he'd savor the chance to extend his reach beyond the Black Hats, and Hyman, Tsigounis, and me—and a field full of cows."

"A field full of cows?" Seeburger asked.

"Never mind, Dick: it's a private joke. By damn, Robertson would love the part."

Margot asked. Robertson accepted. Then the cast began to mushroom. Robertson suggested he should have a side-kick: "You know, Keen, every hero needs a Sancho Panza. Richard will be mine. He shall wear a derby and carry a mace nearly as tall as he is. I, the well-dressed devil, shall wear a top hat and tails." Richard's role was written in. The Purdy campus that was about to be invaded needed a president, a pompous one to live up to the reality of the role as we knew it, played out endlessly in huff and puff and rock and roll by President Edel. Bob Singdahlsen huffed and puffed, rocked and rolled and got the job. Rock and roll? Well, then, we needed a guitarist to play those rhythms and a dance number of devils doing their thing.

Margot prevailed on me to join in. I accepted the part of James Dean, a recent entrant of Hell, and tried to do Dean-like gestures in a dance production. I spoke one line at a fleeing angel fallen from Purdy: "Drag you for beers, baby." I could handle that.

Our intuitions were accurate. *Shades of Hades* was a hit, favorably compared by longtime Follies aficionados to *The Sphinx Winks.* Even the set won a round of applause. Remembering that in our first meetings in Bosler Chapel we'd stared at the jingoistic lines of John Henry Newboldt, "This is the chapel: here, my son,/Your father thought the thoughts of youth," the writers (or was it the set designers?) embraced the parody, "This is the snack bar, here, my son,/Your father felt..." not the desire to bleed out in some foreign land but, perhaps, the urge to undermine the coyness of the lovely Susquehanna maidens and the Daisies floated our way from New England, Baltimore, and the Main Line.

Charlie Mayer wrote most of the music. It was spot-on! I collaborated with him and with Bill Haupt on a new finale. Year after year, the Follies had ended with a version of Ham Neely's original finale, "How Did You Like the Show?" There was a movement to replace it, so Bill Haupt and I wrote a new one. Margot and the others accepted it; but then they added Ham Neely's finale to the end of ours. His was a spirit we couldn't shake loose from the show.

Ham Neely was gone from Dickinson Law School by the time I got to college, but I did meet the famous guy in my junior year. It was really kind of spooky. I was alone one afternoon in the basement of Denny Hall. There was a piano there that I sometimes used when I didn't want to bother my fraternity brothers or be bothered by them. None of the ROTC lads, the other users of the basement, was around. I was working on ideas for *Jamaican Jaunt*, the show we would put on in the spring. A short, kind of roly-poly man came into the room looking like a leftover Ivy Leaguer. He was wearing one of those suit coats that buttoned all the way up and had little or no shoulder padding, giving him a pear-shaped appearance. The buttons were straining—about to pop. The knot of a tie peeked out above the top button. The clothes looked as if they might have been expensive. They also looked slept in. His face was jolly and flushed, and his hairline was receding. "Who are you, sitting there at my piano?" he asked. "And what are you up to?"

"I'm Bill Keen," I replied: "and I'm working on songs for the Follies."

"The Follies! Yield the stool, young man: I'll show you the Follies."

I didn't ask him who he was. I didn't need to: I'd already guessed. He played "She's Coming Down the Nile." I sang along.

"How do you know this song? You couldn't have been here then. Don't tell me you were."

"No, I wasn't here then; Hitchner used to play it."

"You know Hitchner? Where's Hitchner now?

"Yeah, I know Ken; we're fraternity brothers."

"Betas, huh?

"Yeah, Betas. But I don't know where he is. He left last year to join the army, and neither of us is much of a letter-writer."

"Did he graduate first?"

"No."

"He probably never will."

"Why not?"

"The Follies." All the while he'd been doodling on the keys, playing tunes I'd learned from Hitchner. A senior woman I recognized from the chorus of *Bachelors' Bend* came into the room, lured there, I suspected, by familiar sounds. Ham Neely was playing How Did You Like the Show? The chorus girl and I belted it out. How cool was this? A meeting that just dropped out of the sky, I thought. But it was getting late, and the Betas shut the door on dinner at six p.m. sharp; so I said my farewells and started to leave. Ham Neely hollered after me, "I'll try to make the show next spring."

"Great," I said, and left. He didn't make it back for *Jamaican Jaunt,* failing to see Dutch and Doug in their big roles. As far as I know, that evening was his last visit to Dickinson. He and the chorus girl sang on. I hope they made the most of it.

CHAPTER EIGHT

We're Still in the Planning Stages: Final Acts at Dear Old D-son

There were several events of my final year that complicated my feelings about Dickinson, some of them positive but others anything but. Let's get the negative doo-doo out of the way first. Girls—I'd caught up to one I really liked, and for a semester we dated regularly. When I told her my feelings and my hope that we'd have a future after I graduated, she asked what I was going to do for a living. My telling her the truth—that I didn't know but it didn't bother me because I was certain I'd find something to work at—clearly bothered her. She was being practical, and that ended that. Then I dated several other girls, but in my continuing unhappiness over being dumped, I fumbled the ball and hurt their feelings in the process.

Other negative events, ones that hurt people I knew and respected, fed in me a growing distrust of the administration, particularly President Edel. The president and some members of the board of trustees had backed down on the decision not to renew Bert Davis's contract. Thus, the best of all my teachers at Dickinson returned, and I was able to benefit from his intelligence, kindness, and understanding in the *three* courses I took with him in my senior year. But the strength of Bert Davis's character was now known more widely than before the administration had stupidly fired him. I probably should have guessed that other institutions would sense his quality and that one of them would hire him away from us.

Undoubtedly the darkest event of my college career occurred over the break between semesters. Walter Sandercock, a junior in Beta Theta Pi and one of my close friends, committed suicide. Walter and I had been glee club and Follies buddies for two and a half years. I'd written a song for him to sing as Reggie in *Jamaican Jaunt*. And we'd played a lot of IF football together.

Walter and I ran into one another on the last day of fall semester finals. I'd had a late final in an econ course, and Walter, who'd been taking a course in the law school, had just finished that exam. He came into the house late in the afternoon, just as I, the only one still there, was about to leave for Harrisburg. He was clearly down in the dumps. He told me he thought he'd just failed the law course. Feeling he'd done worse than he had was typical of Walter; but I could see he really needed some cheering up. I changed my plans, said

I was hungry, and asked him to join me for dinner at the Carlisle Diner.

Walter agreed, we hopped in my car, and I drove downtown. We ate. Walter told me his tale and worried about the disappointment for his father, a lawyer looking forward to having his son join the practice in Penn Argyll. I tried to cheer him up by reminding him of times in the past when he'd thought he'd really messed up and then come out of the semester with a higher average than I'd ever made. As we ate and talked, his mood, I thought, was improving; but when we'd finished and I'd driven him back to Conway, where he was living at the time, he implored me to stick around for a while. "C'mon, Bill, let's go back to the house; you can play the piano, and we'll sing some Follies songs."

We sang songs from *Jamaican Jaunt,* including Reggie's (Walter's) solo, with its gag line, "Good Old Reading Beer." Walter went right down the scale and rumbled away on the low note. The singing seemed to be lifting his mood. He definitely seemed in better spirits as he challenged me to a game of ping-pong. It was after nine, and I had a forty-minute drive ahead of me. I begged off: "Hey, man, I've got to get going; see you next week."

"OK, Bill: so long."

A week later, I left Harrisburg at nine in the morning to drive back for a midmorning econ class, the first of my final semester. By the time I got to Carlisle and approached the campus, I was running a bit late, so I parked on High Street near Denny Hall and joined some other stragglers. As I climbed the steps into Denny, I overheard a coed say to her friend, "…the Beta who killed himself."

"Who killed himself?" I blurted out. She turned, and recognizing me, said, "Oh, Bill, you don't know? Walter Sandercock hanged himself in his room in Conway."

"He did what?"

"Hanged himself. The janitor found him. He'd been dead for several days."

I stumbled around Denny and, simply by accident, found the room where Dr. Prentice was holding his econ class. I don't remember a thing he said. When the class was over, I walked back to the Beta house, forgetting that I'd parked my car down by Denny. Later, when I didn't see my car in its usual spot, I remembered leaving it down there. It took me some time to overcome my reticence to walk back for it, past Conway Hall where Walter had been living, down to the steps of Denny where I'd heard he was dead.

Sometimes the deity seems to know when you've had enough and sends you a sunny day. Indeed, in those troubling times, there were several more positive events—an A in Romantic poetry from Bert Davis, the rollicking success of *Shades of Hades,* successful glee club concerts on campus and in Philadelphia and Washington DC, and, of course, good times with Robertson and Richard, Paul Brown, and

Bob Singdahlson. Then, at the time Bert Davis told me he wouldn't be coming back, he handled my disappointment by taking several long afternoons talking with me about my future. I remember this important experience even after all these years.

He told me he'd been happy to teach me, that I had improved remarkably in the three years he'd known me. Well, I guess so. The first paper I'd written for him back in the sophomore survey course had earned me a D; by the end of that semester I'd managed to make a B-. After that, I'd always made at least a B. In my senior year I made an A in the Romantics course, a B+ in Victorians, and a B+ in the independent study he'd arranged for me and supervised when he discovered I wasn't eligible for honors. To do a senior honors project, a student needed pretty close to a 3.00 overall. Then we'd talked about another way, the independent study.

He asked me if I had an interest I'd like to spend some time on. A year earlier, when Bert discovered I wasn't one of the prep school students who'd had instruction in analysis of poetic form, he'd given me a book, Laurence Perrine's *Sound and Sense,* and recommended two others, Brooks and Warren's *Understanding Poetry* and Brooks's *The Well Wrought Urn.* I cut a lot of other classes while I schooled myself in new critical close reading and the characteristics and development of poetic forms.

Yes, I told him, I wanted to study how a particular poetic form had developed over time. What had led me in this direction, in addition to *Sound and Sense* and the work of Brooks and Warren, were the classes during the Romantics course when Bert Davis had talked about how sonnets, Keats's own and his predecessors', had influenced the form of his odes. Also, I knew that, beginning in 1557, with *Tottel's Miscellany*, English writers had begun to develop a number of versions of the sonnets written by their Italian predecessors. Indeed, in Bert Davis's sophomore survey course, we'd compared Italian, English, and Spenserian sonnets. I told him I wanted to know more about sonnets and how the varieties had developed over time. He led me back to Tottel's *Miscellany* and the two volumes of Sidney Lee's *Elizabethan Sonnets*. He asked me to get right down to business and try to finish my paper soon after spring vacation, because, with his upcoming move, he'd be extremely busy before the end of the semester.

Every night after selling sandwiches I'd retreat to the Beta dining room and read, analyze, compare, and categorize hundreds of examples of one of the richest forms of England's golden age. The results of this most sustained academic endeavor of my life was a paper of more than forty pages, and yeah, if I'd had more time—the three weeks that were still left in the semester, for instance—I could have made it shorter. Bert Davis read it. He said I clearly had learned how to deal with sonnets. The paper, he judged, was worth a B+.

If I'd had had time to edit it down to size, it could have been an A. I was happy with a B+. Yeah, I know, the records at Dickinson didn't include pluses and minuses; but Bert Davis's grades, penned on the actual papers, did.

During the time I was working on sonnets and conferring with Bert Davis almost every week, he began to question me about my future. I still didn't have any definite plans. I knew I didn't want to be drafted into the armed services or work for an insurance company, which was where a lot of English majors were headed. I told him I'd thought about high school teaching, but that the education courses I'd taken had dampened my enthusiasm; and, anyway, I hadn't started in on them early enough to do the practice-teaching part. To continue, I'd have to come back to college for another year. My father wasn't going to listen to that.

"Well, Bill, what do you like to do?" Bert asked.

"I like to read and write and play sports; and, though I've not traveled much, I'd like to see the world."

"I suggest you do consider teaching—teaching English. You'll read and write; and if you save your money, you'll have summers to travel, and," he added, "there are other avenues than the public schools. I've heard that you're a decent athlete; look into prep schools. They don't require certification to begin teaching, and they often hire teachers who can also coach the students in one or more sports."

"Yes, sir, I've considered that; but Heber Harper advised me to be careful, because prep schools want you to live in a dorm and proctor the boys. I've had enough of living with the boys here at Dickinson."

"Heber Harper should know what he's talking about," Bert replied. "So, here's another way: you could apply for a graduate assistantship at a university and work for a master's degree. You wouldn't have to pay tuition and the school would pay you a stipend for the teaching you'd do. It wouldn't be a princely wage, but you could live on it. Many of us have. If you are interested," he added, "we'll have to act fast."

I was interested. He had available application forms that had been sent to the English department by graduate programs looking for students. He chose from the schools the ones he thought I might get into: Columbia, his own graduate school; Duke; University of Pennsylvania; and Lehigh. "Take these with you, Bill, fill them out, and get them back to me as soon as you can. I'll write letters of recommendation for you and suggest they waive application fees. You'll need to have letters from at least one other professor."

"Professor Warlow."

"Good. Frank's doing his work at Penn. Ask him to write for you and stress that we'll need the letters as soon as he can get them done."

I filled out the forms, requested the letters, picked them up a couple of days later, and mailed them off. On the way back from the post office, I stopped by Robertson's apartment and found him home reading *A Farewell to Arms*. We both dug Hemingway, and Robertson actually had a beard that might have been competitive down in Cuba. Yeah, you could still go to Cuba in those days. Uncharacteristically, I was rousting him away from a book. "Robertson, let's go have a beer: I'm buying."

He frowned up from behind the pages.

"OK. A scotch or a gimlet," I said.

"You're on, Keen; let us go then, you and I, to the James Wilson Hotel when the afternoon is laid out across the sky…"

"God, how literary can you get?"

Several weeks passed before the letters from the graduate schools began to arrive. Columbia wasn't interested, nor was Penn. Duke said that I could come to Durham and try. I'd have to pay a fee, and their best offer of a job was "possibly after a successful semester in the program." Yeah, graduate school was a long shot. I'd finish my courses, spend time with my friends, walk across the stage with the rest of my class, go home to Harrisburg, and regroup. There'd been a lot of rain that spring. A rocky relationship I'd been in with a young woman who'd also be graduating had come to an end. No, the truth? I ended it, not very gracefully. We were headed in different directions. The Dickinson health service didn't employ a shrink. I could have used one.

It was the day before our graduation. The seniors were returning to campus after a week's vacation following final exams. Some of us had joined Ted Auman at his cottage in Brandt Beach, New Jersey. I remember driving back to Carlisle with Dutch Skeel in his old convertible, wondering whether anything interesting was going to happen; or whether the whole experience would wind down in some dispirited way. We got back to Carlisle at dusk. Dutch dropped me at the house and left, not saying where he was headed.

The fraternity house was deserted. I spent an hour or so making sure I'd collected all my things. I loaded most of the stuff in Heap II, a 1949 Chevy that had replaced my original sandwich business car for my senior year. What I couldn't cram in, Pappy could haul back to Harrisburg after the ceremony the next day.

Since there was nothing going on at the house, I started to walk down to the Jimmie for a beer. Reaching the corner and waiting for the light to change, I noticed some activity down the street at the Phi Kap and Phi Ep houses. I thought I'd probably be welcome at one or the other, but I knew I wouldn't be very good company. Then, crossing High Street from the direction of those fraternities, I met a senior woman I knew well enough to greet by name. "Hello, Gretta, where have you been?"

"Oh, I was down there at a dismal fraternity party where too much beer was leading to some last-minute desperate groping. I've drunk enough and seen more than enough, so I'm going back to Drayer. What about you, Bill?"

" I'm at loose ends. I don't know where my friends are. There's no one back at our house. I thought I'd walk around Carlisle one last time, maybe stop in at the Jimmie or Frychland's."

"Mind if I join you in the walking part?"

"Not at all, but where's your guy, the law student?"

"We're having a vacation from one another."

"What do you mean? Have you broken up?"

"Nothing like that; we're just taking some time off from one another."

"Well, sure, if he doesn't mind and you don't mind, come walk with me." We walked toward Drayer and then past the dorm toward Fryckland's.

When we were approaching that water hole, Gretta said, "Bill, let's not go in there; why don't we just walk some more?"

"Fine with me, Gretta." We walked to the right down the street where Creigton Reed had switched the street sign and gotten himself, Bill Corey, and me hauled into the Carlisle police station.

We talked as we walked, mostly by mouthing clichés. "What will you be doing next year, Bill?"

"I don't know, Gretta. Professor Davis thinks I should go to graduate school; but I haven't had any positive news from the five I applied to. Duke would allow me to enter, but I'd have to pay my own way. That's not going to happen. What about you, Gretta? I heard you might be getting married soon. Is that so?"

"I'm not sure. My engagement has been an on-again, off-again thing. I'm not sure. So I'll be going to New York and preparing myself to be an executive secretary. If I do marry, I can run my husband's law office."

"That sounds like good planning, Gretta. I hope everything works out."

"Maybe it will, maybe it won't; but if you're coming to New York next year, get in touch with me. I'll be staying at the Barbizon Hotel for Women. You like musical comedies, don't you?"

"Indeed I do! Gretta, I haven't got even a hint where I'll be; but if I land anywhere near New York, I will get in touch with you."

By this time, we'd walked around the sides of a long block and were heading across the campus toward the back of Drayer, giving the rocks where lovers were wont to lie a wide berth. We approached the dorm where lovers were wont to bid one another the sweetest of dreams, as some were doing on that very night. We arrived at the steps of Drayer. "Gretta," I said; "I've enjoyed our walk and our talk." I held out my hand to shake; after all, she was engaged.

"Oh, Bill," she said, leaning forward and kissing me.

I wasn't expecting it; but I was hoping it might happen.

She turned and went up the steps to the front door of Drayer. Before she went in, she turned and smiled down at me: "See you in New York, Bill."

I didn't know what to say.

As I walked back High Street toward the Beta house, I was having complicated feelings. The roar of a motorcycle announced the arrival of Robertson. "Keen, you old stick, where have you been? You've missed my party. I even sent Takacs to find you, but he came back empty-handed."

"I was walking around the streets of Carlisle, Robertson."

"Walking, Keen, why on earth would you be walking when your presence was needed at my party?"

"I like to walk around Carlisle because it's flat. I figured tonight might be my last chance, at least for a while."

"Well, hop on the back, Keen: we still have time to refresh ourselves at the James Wilson."

"No thanks, Robertson. I'm done for tonight. I'm going to bed."

"Oh, Keen, you have turned into an incredibly old stick."

"Yeah, I know."

"Well, then, famous sandwich man, when shall we two meet again?"

"I don't know, Robertson; but you know where I live when I'm at home."

"Yes, and you know where I live. So come for a visit and we'll ride through the Poconos."

"We'll see, Robertson: we'll see."

Too early the next morning, Pappy invaded the Beta house and rousted me out of bed. "C'mon, Bill; you've got to go graduate. Your mother, Marion, Barbie, and Jim are waiting outside in the car. Don't forget to thank your Aunt Marion for helping out."

How could I forget? I said to myself.

III

"GO TELL IT ON THE MOUNTAIN"

CHAPTER ONE

The Waiting Game:
Patience or Procrastination?

I was back in Harrisburg, not much to do, nowhere to go. I slept a lot. When I finally made it downstairs most days, it was nearly noon. For a week, when I was awake, I spent the days reading *Moby Dick*. When Pappy got home in the evenings, he'd ask me if I'd started to look for a job.

"No, I haven't."

Then he grumbled something about the jobs listed in the *Patriot*. Being a morning paper, it'd been lying around all day. "You majored in English. You can read the newspaper, can't you?"

I hadn't bothered to flip through it. Sure, I could read the newspaper, but I figured that looking for my vocation in the Harrisburg papers would be as useless as applying to graduate school had been.

Then we went on vacation. I tried to beg off, but my mother insisted. She'd arranged to spend a week with Aunt Jane and Uncle Donald and their kids at a cabin on Lake James in Indiana. Barbie was excited because she'd be able to spend time with Nancy Pat, her favorite cousin. I don't know what brother Jim—yeah, he'd become Jim by then—I don't know what Jim thought. He was going, whether he wanted to or not. I was going too. At least I could put off the job search for a bit .

The fact is I don't remember much about that vacation. We ate our way through a whole cooked ham and drank endless Cokes. Alas, there was no beer. My father managed to cut his eyeball with the edge of the newspaper, and we spent an afternoon in an emergency room. That was the high point. On the way home, in blistering heat on Sideling Hill, Pappy's Pontiac overheated. We lingered by the side of the turnpike until the car cooled, then crept on a couple of miles until it began to boil again. It took us three times as long to get home as it had to get to Indiana. It was very late when we got back to Harrisburg. Aunt Marion, who'd been caring for my grandmother, was already in bed. I tried to sleep in the attic. It was a furnace.

About nine the next morning, after fits and starts of sweating sleep, I came downstairs. It had been a bit cooler there, so Pappy had grabbed the couch. He was reading the *Patriot*. "There's a proofreader's job at the Telegraph Press," he said. We were back to that. I was about to respond when the phone rang. Barbie got there first. I guessed it was Janie Ensmibger or Patty Leftwich or maybe a young swain who fancied her.

"Brother Bill, it's for you."

"Who would be calling me at nine fifteen in the morning?"

"A local farmer who wants you to milk his cows," Pappy quipped from behind the *Patriot*.

"Daddy, don't be silly," Barbie said. "It's Mrs. Sallay from the English department at Lehigh."

Aunt Marion hobbled in from the dining room to announce, "Oh, Bill, I didn't get to tell you. She called yesterday. She wants to offer you a job."

Pappy, who had emerged from the paper, said, "Don't just stand there, Bill; answer the damn phone before she hangs up!"

As it turned out, Mrs. Sallay, secretary to Professor J. Burke Severs, Head of the English Department at Lehigh, speaking for her boss, told me that Professor Severs wanted to offer me a job, a teaching assistantship paying fifteen hundred dollars for two semesters' work and a waiver of the tuition fee. I could begin to work on an MA without borrowing money.

"Yes, I'll accept the appointment. Yes, I'll be there by September 6."

Now I'd even begin to scan the *Patriot* for a summer job. My mother pitched in, calling our neighbor Charlie

Whistler, past president of the school board, who still had some clout. He came through, and I spent six weeks taking the school census. In the evenings, I hung with younger guys in Reservoir Park, the ones who hadn't yet been drafted, and with Milt Thompson and Ronnie Smith, who'd done their time and were beyond all that. Occasionally I'd join Jerry Lego for beer and crab cakes at Suky's Tavern. Jerry had graduated from Lebanon Valley. He was waiting for the draft.

I also spent a lot of time with my father. Again, he was excited for me, at least as excited as he'd been when I'd decided to go to Dickinson. When Pappy had graduated from Penn State, he'd been hired to join the Loop Program at Bethlehem Steel. Its purpose was to turn graduate engineers into practical ones. He'd worked in the Bridge Department, located on the south side of Bethlehem adjacent to the Lehigh campus; and he'd lived in a boardinghouse in Warren Square, just up the street from his work. There he met Fran Trembley, a young member of the Lehigh biology department. Fran was a practical joker and, I suspect, a partier. I wonder if he was a kind of Robertson to my father. The next year Pappy married my mother, and they moved to an apartment in West Bethlehem.

When Pappy talked of those times, of Lehigh football games, of trips to speakeasies, and of the hijinks of Fran Trembley, he'd wax enthusiastic: "You're gonna love it, Bill; lots of great food and sporting events, and if you thought

Dickinson was a park, wait till you see Lehigh! It's built on the side of a mountain, and most of the fraternity houses are near the top in a forest!"

On September 5, 1957, I got to see the place for myself. We arrived in the early afternoon so Pappy would have time to drive me through the campus on a winding road that eventually brought us to a lookout where we could gaze down on the industrial valley, the location of Bethlehem Steel. He pointed out the library, Packard Lab, and Grace Hall, where the wrestling matches would be held, and the football field where the Engineers would play and I'd get to see them play Lafayette in the most frequently contested football rivalry of all the colleges and universities.

After the tour, we found Muschlitz Street, not much more than a paved goat path heading up the mountainside at a hair-raising angle. That's where I'd be living for the first year. As he helped me cart my stuff into the house, I could have sworn he thought he was coming back to Bethlehem, to a time when his dreams were still reaching into the future.

CHAPTER TWO:

Setting to Work in a New World: Year One at Lehigh

On the morning of September 6, I set out to find some breakfast and then Christmas-Saucon Hall, the building where I'd be spending most of my time teaching classes and keeping office hours. I'd read the introductory material Mrs. Sallay had sent. Christmas-Saucon Hall was near the bottom of the campus, which meant that it was only halfway up the steep hill of New Street from its lowest point at the Lehigh River. It would be downhill all the way from Muschlitz Street—a good thing, too, because, after that, nearly everywhere I had to go on campus involved a climb, beginning right inside the entrance to Christmas-Saucon, where seemingly endless stairs rose to the English Department.

I found the center of the English world on the third floor, but you could think it was more than that because the ceilings of the first two floors were high ones. When you got up there, you could look out at its massive neighbor, the Lehigh Chapel. I later discovered, in mild weather, I could open my office window and listen to an organ concert or the beautiful sounds of the Bethlehem Bach Choir.

On that first day, I had arrived early, my required meeting not being until after lunch. Yeah, I was eager to get started: and I wanted to case the joint before I settled in. I stood in the doorway of the office and saw a smiling older woman, older than my mother—maybe a grandmother—sitting behind a large desk. "Hello, may I help you?" she said.

"Hello," I replied. "I'm William Keen—I know I'm early, but…"

"Oh, Mr. Keen, please come in. I'm Mrs. Sallay. We've been talking on the phone. Yes, you are early, but that's fine, because Professor Severs is in his office, and I don't think he's busy right now. Just let me ring him." She rang him, had a brief conversation, and led me up into his office. Yes, up into his office, which adjoined the outer office I'd been standing in but was two steps higher than it and everything else in the English Department, as I would soon discover. Why not, Professor Severs was the head of the whole operation. Mrs. Sallay led me up and introduced me to the Man In Charge.

"Ah, Mr. Keen, welcome. Please have a seat. I'm glad you dropped by early. Yes-ah, we can have a nice chat."

I sat looking at Professor Severs, a man in his late fifties, by my guess, with a slightly receding hairline and a trimmed mustache. He was wearing wire-framed glasses with very round lenses that made him look every bit the internationally recognized Chaucer scholar I knew him to be. I'd been reading the material. He asked if I'd moved in and was ready to go. I said I was.

"Well, then, ah, since Mr. Hartung will be explaining your teaching duties at the second meeting this afternoon, suppose we talk about the courses, ah, you will be taking. Four graduate seminars are being offered this semester. You will be taking two, ah."

Professor Severs guided me toward Alexander Pope, taught by Mr. Dilworth, and Colonial American Literature, taught by Mr. Emerson. I was happy about the first, having studied Pope with Bert Davis at Dickinson. About the second, I hadn't a clue. Aside from reading Hemingway on my own, I'd had very little contact with American literature. I think I was surprised that there was such a course as Colonial American Literature; but what the hell, they were going to let me do it for nothing. Better still, they were going to pay me to teach, fifteen hundred dollars! How about that! I liked the idea of a paying job, even though I had no idea how to do it. Well, I'd have two years to find out.

As it happened, I didn't need two years to discover what I should be working at. It took me part of the first semester, which I spent fumbling around in *The Province of Prose,* trying to stimulate discussion of the essays, reading my students' weekly themes, writing comments in the margins of their drafts, and urging them to rewrite, again and again and maybe again. Then, as I read theme number nine and discovered that my students were actually learning how to write decent prose, I felt a surge of pride for them and for my role in their accomplishments. But on September 6, 1957, what I would learn about myself by teaching others was still in the future. I needed to go to meetings, settle into my own studies, and meet some people. I had a week to do that before the first classes.

At the first meeting that afternoon, I began to meet people—professors I'd probably be taking courses with; other graduate students, nervous new ones like myself and more experienced ones who offered to talk about ways of teaching the essays. In freshman English, all the sections were on the same schedule of reading and writing assignments; that was a boon to the beginner, however boring it might become for any teacher who lingered too long at that level.

The second meeting, run by Al Hartung (he said "Call me Al" and I did), was only for the teaching assistants. He handed out copies of *The Province of Prose* and *The Century Handbook,* a day-by-day syllabus of reading and writing assignments, a sheet of room assignments, and grade books, and told us we'd be meeting once a week to discuss teaching techniques and practice grading themes. "Total uniformity in grading is probably impossible to achieve," he said, "but by grading themes in a group and discussing our evaluations,

we aim to come as close to agreement as possible." He scheduled our next meeting and excused the veterans. "New men,
follow me." He led us back to Mrs. Sallay's office, where we
were shown where our mail boxes were located and given
keys to the building and our offices. My office was just two
doors down the hall. I'd be sharing it with Frank Behrens,
another beginner.

While Frank Behrens and I were settling in, Calvin Israel,
one of the veteran TAs I'd seen at the earlier meeting, came
in and struck up a conversation with Frank Behrens: "Al
tells me you're from City College, Frank." Frank was. So was
Calvin. They talked about professors they'd both had. "And
what about you...ah...William?"

"Bill, please; just plain Bill."

"OK, Bill. And I'm just plain Calvin." We shook hands.

"Where did you go to college, Bill?"

"I went to Dickinson, Calvin."

"Oh, over in Carlisle. Good school, good school."

"It had its moments," I said.

"Aha, sounds as if there's a tale to tell."

"There just might be."

Then, addressing both of us new guys, he said, "Well,
look, Al doesn't like long meetings, so he didn't tell you everything you might want to know."

"In my case," I said, "that might take a while."

"Good point," Frank Behrens snorted.

Calvin Israel was loaded with information he was eager to share: "First things first. In addition to Christmas-Saucon, the most important building on campus is the library. Do you know where it is?"

Frank nodded a yes. I said, "Yes, it's up the hill."

"True," Calvin said, "but practically everything at Lehigh is up the hill. How about the English Seminar Room—do you know where that is?"

Frank looked as if he didn't; I said, "Nope."

"If you're ready for a hike, I'll show you."

Frank begged off; he had other plans. I said, "Let's go." We left Christmas-Saucon and hiked up the hill to the library and then up to the third floor. I didn't see any elevators. Just getting from one place to another at Lehigh should earn you phys ed credit.

The English Seminar Room was at the end of a hallway. On its far side you could look down the hill to Christmas-Saucon and beyond to the South Side. On the opposite wall, you could find all the books that had been put on reserve for the seminars being offered. There were loads of books for Colonial American Literature—Calvin's *Institutes, The Westminster Confessions,* and a shitload of sermons. For Pope, there was the standard multivolume edition.

In the center was a long table—actually three tables pushed together to make one long one—and fifteen or so captain's chairs. Three of them were already occupied by students reading books and scribbling notes; they were too busy to look up from their work. Calvin and I left. In the hallway just outside the English Seminar Room was a door which, Calvin explained, opened into the stacks very close to where the relevant periodicals were shelved. Finding it locked, like a magician, he—*presto!*—produced a key. "You'll need one of these to avoid a fifteen-mile hike every time you need to read an article in a journal. And believe me, there'll be lots of times. I'll get you one."

"Thanks, Calvin."

Back outside in front of the library, Calvin asked, "What else can I tell you, Bill?"

"Can you recommend good places to eat that don't cost too much?"

"For lunch, right up there in Packer Hall." He pointed up at a large building on the next level up from the library. "There's a good snack bar with hot soups and sandwiches, and cheap daily specials. That's where the graduate students who don't brown bag it usually eat lunch. The college bookstore, a post office, and the infirmary are also in Packer Hall. For dinner, well, there are restaurants down the hill on Fourth Street. Try the New Merchant's Hotel. It's on the corner of Fourth and New. The specials are eighty-five cents; so, with the tip, you're in and out for a dollar."

I hadn't had any lunch, so when Calvin said so long and headed home, I walked downhill to the New Merchant's.

The dining room was open but empty. So I went into the bar and had a draft beer. Actually, I had several drafts while I waited. For a couple of evenings, I ate dinner there. I got lunch at the snack bar, and spent most of the morning and afternoon reading the assignments for the first meeting of Colonial American Literature. Mr. Emerson had put a long list in my mailbox in Christmas-Saucon Hall. Calvin's *Institutes.* Gag! Maybe I should have interviewed with insurance companies.

Usually I found two others laboring on assignments—Jasper Collura and John Gustavson. Collura was very serious and not a talker. Gustavson picked up the slack, whooping to get our attention when he found something ridiculous in one of the puritan sermons.

Late in my first week at Lehigh, I made the challenging hike up past Packer Hall to a higher level of the campus by a steadily rising winding road that brought me to the fraternities. I knew there was a Beta chapter at Lehigh because some of its members had come to Dickinson for a district meeting the year before. Fortunately, it was one of the nearer ones, the fourth, I think, that I came to. Cars were parked in the driveway and along the road before the house, including a VW bug, a couple of sporty-looking numbers, and one vintage woody station wagon, which was being unloaded by a tall blond guy. "Hello there," I said, "I'm Bill Keen, a Beta from Dickinson."

"Hey, I'm Gil Cowan; grab that case of beer out of the back seat and we'll go rip a few open while I introduce you to the brothers."

I did that. In the living room, I began to meet the brothers, who apparently thought it was time for a break and a beer. Dick Gaintner, an enthusiastic lad with a vigorous handshake, had to be some kind of officer. Right on, he was the chapter president, a premed from Lancaster. I said I'd run on the track there. The conversation was up and running.

I told the brothers I was a graduate student in English and that I had a room nearby (if you went across country from Muschlitz Street to the Beta house, you could cut out some of the hills).

"Where are you taking your meals?" Steve Gartside asked.

"Here and there," I said. "I think I've got breakfast and lunch covered, but I was wondering if I could arrange for dinner here."

"Absolutely, we can work that out. You'll have to get through the weekend, because we don't start serving meals until Monday."

"Thanks, I look forward to it. Do you guys sing at meals?"

"You can bet on it, man, we're Betas!"

I was glad I'd climbed up the hill. During that first year at Lehigh, in addition to eating dinners at the Beta house, I attended most of their parties and joined them for football games and wrestling matches—a sport I quickly glommed on to. The Betas had more varsity wrestlers than any other fraternity—Dick Santoro, Bob Gunst, Leon Harbold, and Eddie Hamer, who won a national championship; and there were several others who had wrestled in prep school. I actually worked out with a couple of them and found I was hard to take down because of my low center of gravity. For a brief time in junior high school, I'd wrestled at the Y; but the sport wasn't contested in Harrisburg schools in those days. Oh, well, you can't do everything.

Classes started up and I was busier than I'd ever been. I walked into the first section of composition I was to teach and found eighteen students. Several of them had to be veterans, because they looked at least my age or older. I steadied my nerves by calling the roll. Fortunately, the first day had been scripted for the new teachers by Al Hartung: we were to call the role; introduce ourselves; and hand out the syllabus, pointing out the review of grammar we'd get to right away, the readings in *The Province of Prose,* and the nearly weekly compositions—the prepared themes and the impromptus. To encourage uniformity in grading, the department used four exchange themes, so called because they would be read by someone other than the instructor. The first of these was the fourth paper. It was supposed to tune up the students and the new instructors for the rigors of "objective" grading. The final three papers, all impromptus graded by other teachers, were called the "hurdles." A student who had a passing average both in the first nine themes and the final three themes passed the course. A student who failed both parts failed outright. A student who failed one part or the other had his work reviewed by one of the veteran teachers; about a third of the students whose work was reviewed were given passes. The failing students retook the course, some more than once. It would be fair to say that the composition program was respected by some and feared, even hated, by many.

Following the example set for me by Alan McGill at Dickinson, I encouraged students to confer with me and to rewrite their papers, though the department required only local revisions in spelling, mechanics, and grammar. I was very busy, busier, I think, than the other TAs who opted for the route of minor revision. When the final grades were in, if I remember correctly, none of my students had failed.

Most of the rest of the daylight hours were spent in the English Seminar Room, reading the primary texts and the important secondary scholarship that had been amassed on the "reserve shelves" in the seminar room. Monday evening from seven to ten and Saturday morning from nine to twelve, the seminars I was taking met in that same room. I still dream about it—the captain's chairs; the long table; the casement windows; the A and B closets, in one of which copies of the former head's ill-fated *Shelley Legend* were stowed; and the cloud of pipe and cigarette smoke that arose each day from the nearly unanimous addiction of students and professors. By that time I was one of them, having remained pure of lung only for the first semester at Dickinson.

About a month into the semester, on a week when there wasn't a home football game, Ben Gates, Frank Eck, and several other brothers were going to New York in search of some nightlife. They asked me to join them; I could help pay for the gas. As it turned out, I did more than that. Remembering that Gretta Zsaban was in New York, I told the guys I might be able to arrange for some company. When we got to New York and found a lively bar in the Village, the German American Club, on a chance, I called the Barbizon Hotel and—whatta you know?—I was able to reach Gretta. She wasn't out on a date, she knew the club I was calling from, and she would take a cab to it, but she'd be coming alone because none of her friends were there that weekend. I told the guys; they said I should stay at the German American Club to meet Gretta while they did a pub crawl. They'd come back for me later.

Gretta arrived. "Well, I got to New York, Gretta, so I called, as you said I should."

"I'm glad you did, Bill." As it turned out, she and the lawyer were in off-again mode. She asked about Lehigh, how I liked it, and how I was doing in my classes. Lehigh was fine, and I was doing OK. I'd been welcomed by the Betas, so I wasn't as much at sea as some of the graduate students.

"You always were a gung-ho fraternity boy."

"Not so much as I used to be, but it's good to be with a gang that sings the songs I know."

"You always were a good singer."

"Thanks, I'll keep trying to be."

"I've never been to Lehigh, but I've heard about the Lehigh parties from girls at Katherine Gibbs."

"Well," I said, following her lead and delivering my speech in one onward-rushing breath: "Fall house party is two weeks from now, Friday through Sunday; and I'd like you to be my guest. There's a train from New York to Bethlehem, or you can take a bus; and the dates get to stay in the house while the brothers sleep elsewhere around town. The ladies are protected by a formidable crew of older women sometimes referred to as the Wombats."

"I'll check the train and bus schedules. Do you have a phone?"

"Not a personal one, but you can call me at the English Department during my office hours, ten to eleven Monday, Wednesday, and Friday mornings." I gave her the number.

We spent the evening sipping beers and talking about our lives since Dickinson. It hadn't been that long, but it seemed as if one hell of a lot had happened.

On Friday afternoon of Fall House Party weekend, I met Gretta at the railroad station and drove her around the town and the campus in a borrowed car, ending up at the Beta house in time for her to register, find her room, and freshen up before the initial event, a cocktail party on the back porch of the house that overlooked the lower campus. She met again Ben Gates and Frank Eck, and I introduced her to Gil Cowan and Dick Gaintner. Gaintner joked about discovering that the young professor could attract such a good-looking woman. Gretta cooed and flirted.

We had dinner at the house—quite a spread, with a variety of cheeses, shrimp, standing rib of beef, and a choice of wines. I should say that, ordinarily, the food was decent enough; but this was a special event for which all the brothers participating, including me, would pay a special fee. Why not? House Party weekends happened only twice a year, and many of the guys were entertaining their best girls, brought from miles away, rather than relying on the local girls from Cedar Crest, Moravian, and St. Luke's Nursing School.

After dinner, a combo of Lehigh students, one of them a Beta, appeared and played cool jazz, easy dancing music—"Lullaby of Birdland," "September in the Rain," and "Satin Doll," even though at Lehigh in 1958 there were no satin dolls. Yeah, it was about as lilly-white as Dickinson. Gretta and I danced. Actually, Gretta danced a lot, a few times with me and a lot with Ben Gates and other suave movers. I wasn't entirely out of it, because I got to dance with their dates. It was a mild evening for autumn, so some couples repaired to the porch, where, at dusk, you could look down on the lights of the lower campus gleaming up at you like a string of pearls adorning the queen of the ball. As an antidote to Cotton Mather's sermons and *The History of the Dividing Line*, I had been reading F. Scott Fitzgerald's Princeton novel, *This Side of Paradise*. On a big weekend, Lehigh could compete with the Ivy League, as the Engineers did on the gridiron and in wrestling. This was long before the creation of the Patriot League, the Ivy League wannabe. Anyhow, the gentle weather and the lights on the campus were doing their thing, and Gretta and I were feeling close. Then, she broke the mood—I'm sure she didn't mean to, but that's what happened when she said, "You know, Bill, my engagement isn't set in stone; I could break it off if you wanted…"

I cut her off. "Gretta, we've had several good times together, but I'm in no position to step into your life. At the very soonest, I'll have my MA a year and a half from now; and all sorts of people, professors and other graduate students, have already been working on me to continue on for a PhD. To secure a position and keep it, they tell me, you need a PhD. That'll take at least two additional years of coursework, and who knows how long to pass all the exams and write a dissertation. I don't come from money. My parents can't help me; they've got my sister and brother to see through college. I'm doing graduate work on my own, and it's going to take a while. How long are you willing to wait?"

Gretta had fallen silent while I was pouring forth my lament—and I did lament that I was backing off, pushing away desire as if I had no right to what was, at the very least, a flattering offer from a desirable young woman. We went back inside and sat, saying very little for the rest of the evening. The rest of the weekend was like muted blues—Miles at his saddest. The magic of the campus lights had slipped away into the night.

When we said goodbye the next day at the train station, it was the last time I would see Gretta or hear from her until the following June. Then, the second semester of my graduate course completed, I went home to see my family and to get together at Dickinson with my friends from college.

It was the time of the annual Alumni Weekend that, back then, culminated in Sunday's graduation ceremony. Lots of Betas were there at the house—the current seniors who were about to graduate and a surprisingly large number of guys who'd already graduated and who, like me, were still going to school, most of them in law or medicine. I got more than my share of attention, because Dickinson graduates in English graduate school were rare; and I would more than likely be going on beyond the master's for a PhD. We enjoyed a splendid luncheon banquet prepared by Marion Beyers, the Beta cook; sang Beta songs; and battered one another's ears with exaggerated tales of our successes.

That evening, I walked to Fryckland's with Bob Singdahlsen, who was working for Connecticut General

Insurance Company and had driven a new-to-him convertible back to Carlisle. There we found Margot Patrick and Dick Seeburger, two old Follies friends, and caught up on news of others who hadn't made it back. Robertson and Richard were in Carlisle because both would be graduating on Sunday, Margot said.

It was at Fryckland's that I saw Gretta, who entered the bar with the lawyer, now her husband. I'd heard, earlier in the day, that they'd been married in the spring. I don't know if she'd finished her program in New York. They were standing in the front room near the little horseshoe bar. He was talking to a guy I recognized as a former law student and sandwich patron.

Gretta wasn't participating in the conversation. Rather, she was scanning the crowd in the room. Then she walked away from the lawyers to the archway that led to the back room. I saw her realizing that I was standing there looking at her. She came toward me, but stopped about an arm's length away, turned her head so as to look at me askance, and said, "You know I'm married now, Bill."

"Yes, Gretta, I heard."

"It's great," she said, but she wasn't smiling. She turned and walked back to her husband.

It had been a good year for me at Lehigh. I'd made solid B's in my first-semester courses and again in the second semester—in a seminar on Samuel Johnson's circle with Mr.

Dilworth and one on Whitman and Melville with Professor Strauch. Thanks to Bert Davis, I was well-prepared to deal with eighteenth-century writers. I was soon captivated by the rich humanity of Whitman's poetry. My paper, which looked at several of his poems as realizing his literary-critical thinking, was, according to Professor Strauch, very solid work for a beginner. I was glad I'd impressed him, because he'd certainly impressed me. To discover in texts about Whitman's poetry that the man you were studying with had written a groundbreaking essay—on "Song of Myself"—was a new experience. Bert Davis was a wonderful teacher, but his book on Johnson hadn't yet been published when he was teaching me.

Near the end of May, the courses Lehigh would be offering in the summer were announced—a seminar on Carlyle and Arnold offered by Professor Strauch among them. I talked with Professor Severs. He encouraged me to enroll, adding that the terms of my graduate assistantship made summer study tuition free. That did it. Being frugal, I'd lived on less than I'd made and would be able to make it through the summer and up to the end of September, when I'd receive my first check of the new year.

Having decided to stay and study, I arranged to live at the Beta house that summer—free of charge. Indeed, for several weeks I even ate dinner free of charge by cooking for a gang of six undergrads, another grad student, and myself. Two of the undergrads were victims of the freshman composition course. I tutored them in the manly art of revision. Their improved grades won me a night of clams and beer at the Roosevelt Bar and Grill. Being able to do some successful tutoring made me happy with myself. By that time, I knew that concentrating on an area I was interested in made all the difference. Sure, I still had to shift gears, but now the courses were always about language. I felt at home reading books and writing papers and, of course, revising, revising, revising. What pleased me most, however, was the success I had had teaching my students in the second semester of English composition. Once again, twelve papers were required, prepared and impromptu, with the same hurdles system; but this time, the texts studied were all works of imaginative literature. We started with *The Iliad;* moved up in time to the *Canterbury Tales;* and forged onward to *Hamlet; Twelve Poets* brought us from Shakespeare to the moderns; and *Modern Short Stories* and *Brave New World* kept us there. In addition to the compositions, there were two exams on details from the works. Word got around about whose students had done well on the first exam. My name was mentioned, along with several others.

When we came to the poets, I noticed some uneasiness among the students and an increase in the number coming to me for additional help. I took my time, leading my charges through the arts of paraphrase and explication. As the pace slowed, we didn't always cover all the poems they'd read. I tried to impress on my guys that I was leading them through processes, and that it was up to them to use the processes on poems we hadn't gotten around to. Didn't they have to solve problems on their own in math classes? Sure, but they'd studied math forever; hell, they were training to be engineers. Poetry, they complained, was a strange new beast.

The march of the lemmings to my office continued. On a Monday afternoon, three students showed up; two of them were new to me. "Who are you guys? You looking for Mr. Behrens?" (Frank was still my office mate).

My student answered for them: "These fellas and I live on the same hall. I've been helping them to paraphrase and explicate as you're teaching us to do."

"Yeah," said one of the interlopers, "my TA, Mr...."

"Whoa, no names!"

"Well, uh, our teacher acts as if we were supposed to know how to read poetry before we got here. Didn't teach us any of that at Steelton."

"Hmm, Steelton. I went to John Harris. I wasn't taught how to read poetry either. You guys play football?"

"Yeah."

"Steelton always gave us tough games. I remember Dick Reich kicking our butts." I turned to my student, the budding tutor: "So you've been helping them, Lon?"

"Yeah, but Yeats and Eliot are tough for me."

"I understand. A lot of allusion and what I call jump cuts."

"Jump cuts?"

"I'll explain it later, when we're looking at an example. I'll tell you what. You guys find a meeting room we can use this week. Afternoon or evening better?"

"Evening, the football coach has got both of us out for track."

"How about Thursday evening, seven thirty? That'll give me a chance to talk to my classes on Wednesday. I'll need to know where the room is by then, Lon. I'll announce a volunteer review session on Thursday evening…intended for my classes, but I won't kick out anyone else who shows up. That sound OK?"

"Yes, sir. Thanks so much," Lon said.

"Now don't go quiet on me, Lon. You're going to be a big part of this. How about coming in on Wednesday so we can do some planning?"

"Sure. I was planning on doing that."

"OK. I'll see if I can lure a few of your classmates into the game."

In class on Wednesday, Lon said he'd found a lounge in their dorm, one with couches and easy chairs. There were some folding chairs available, and guys could sit on the floor.

I announced the review session and asked for volunteers to join Lon and me as chief players in the exercise. We'd all get together that afternoon for a practice session. At three,

Lon and two other students, Bob and Jim, showed up. We worked on Yeats's "The Second Coming." Lon was ready to talk about the allusion in the title and behind the rough beast. I said I'd read the poem aloud. "That's how you always start and end. Feel the meter and notice how the meter works along with the grammar of the sentences, the grammatical rhythm, so to speak. Forget about the iambic monotony that gets drummed into your heads in high school, and ask yourselves what the poem tells you about the kind of experience it's presenting with the phrase, "The darkness drops again." I read; they listened and identified the sentences and correctly explained that the poem was presenting a vision fostering a moment of understanding. We talked about epiphanies.

"Good work, guys," I said. Only then did I explain Yeats's theory of history, the interpenetrating gyres. "See it, guys? OK. On Thursday evening we'll work through this poem together. Then I'll split the class into groups, and each of you will employ a similar process to lead a group through "Leda and the Swan." Lon, you explain the myth. Let's run through it." We did. We were ready.

The room was packed. I had to work my way through the mass of bodies sprawled on the floor. The four of us did a job on "The Second Coming"; then the three of them led the rest of the crowd through "Leda." When we had finished, hands shot up. The first one I recognized asked the question I sensed was on its way: "Can we come to your class?"

"Here's a better idea. Get together in groups as you've just done and help one another become sufficient teachers of the rest of the poems." I think I half-convinced them, but I had to promise to meet with them once more and lead them through "Prufrock." Even so, my office hours were crowded, often with new faces.

In the company of Ray Armstrong, a senior professor of poetry who taught me a great deal about the art of explication, I complained that increased student visits to my office were cutting into my paper-grading time, making it necessary to read papers well into the night. He shut me up faster than my father used to: "Ninety-eight percent of the sentient faculty would consider student visits as compliments," he said. Then, casting me a look that implied he might be wasting his breath, he continued with the punchline: "Those visits are the best evidence that there's a fighting chance you might eventually become a teacher."

Touché!

A few days after semester's end, I was in my office doing some filing when the phone rang. "Is this Professor Keen, formerly the famous sandwich man and now prominent university scholar?"

"You bet your ass, R. Blaylock. Where the hell are you?"

"Home, Keen, home. I'll be going back to Carlisle on Thursday; R. Nelson and I will be graduating."

"So I understand. I thought I'd drive back to Carlisle as well. I'll see you there."

"Why wait until then? You can see me tonight. Indeed, I shall drive over to your office in Christmas-Saucon Hall and pick you up. You are to be downstairs outside the building in fifteen minutes. I shall park by the tensile tester." The tensile tester? Well. That's another story. Some people live by the ocean, wafted by sea breezes. Some people live near the top of mountains, fed by wonderful views of rolling hills. The Lehigh English Department lived by the tensile tester, at the time the world's largest device for testing the strength of I-beams, which it did by trying to pull them apart. Each test ended with an earth-shaking WHOMP!

I told the thirsty Robertson, "Make it half an hour; I've got work to finish up."

"Oh, all right, Keen, you old stick."

I was at the appointed place right on time, as was Robertson. He was never late when he was thirsty. He ambled toward me from the parking lot separating Christmas-Saucon from the lab housing the famous tensile tester. He summoned me, "Come forth, Sir William Parker; let us march out in search of liquid refreshment, beer, mead, or usquebaugh. Allow me, longtime resident of this fair industrial valley, to lead you to the most promising establishments. Do you know the inn dubbed the Tallyho?"

"Of course, Robertson, I've been here almost a year. Every Lehigh man knows the Tallyho."

"Well, then, have you ventured forth to the Roosevelt, located in the shadow of the famous Taylor Stadium?"

"Indeed, Robertson. 'Tis a favorite graduate school refreshment spot following upon the conclusion of evening seminars, where we and our beloved professors repair to quaff the golden brew."

"Keen, I must say, your mastery of proper English is improving."

"Why not, me bay-o, oim a gragit stud'en," I came back at him, shifting down a level or two.

"God, Keen, I knew it couldn't last. Where can I take you that you haven't been?" After a moment's thought, "How about Pelligotti's fine establishment in Fountain Hill?"

"Don't know that one, Robertson."

"Good, then thither we shall fare."

"Robertson, what the hell have you been smoking? Sir Walter Raleigh doesn't come in cigars."

"No, Keen, no: I'm still a Wheeling stogie man. I've been reading Shakespeare, not in a course, mind you, but as part of a flirtation with a young lass at Dickinson, an affair that, I fear, has ended; so I have come home to confer with HG about my future. Then I'll be back at Dickinson for frolicking with R. Nelson and picking up my degree."

"Perhaps I will join the romp."

"But now, young squire, let us to Pelligotti's repair, where, word has it, fair maidens of the nursing guild do nightly present themselves, willing, for a drink or two, to share their favors."

"Lead on, R. Blaylock."

Robertson led on to the parking lot, where a shining new black VW bug awaited us.

"What, where's the fabled steed from Deutschland?"

"Garaged, Keen, garaged, with a flattened tire. This replacement is a graduation gift from HG, who thinks an automobile lends an air of maturity appropriate for one who will in September next begin the study of law."

"So I hear. You are about to become dangerous."

"Get in, Keen: we need to drink!"

Robertson drove to Pelligotti's, near St. Luke's Hospital in Fountain Hill. We parked on a side street and walked to the bar. Since it was my first time there, I stopped and took the place in. Someone called my name. I turned and spotted Steve Bird, a fellow graduate student, sitting at a large round booth with three young women—nurses, I guessed. Uncharacteristically, I led Robertson to the booth. "Hello, there," I said to the group; "I'm Bill Keen, and this is my buddy from college, Robertson Taylor."

Questions flew forth from the ladies. "What college? Where you from, Bill? Robertson, don't I know you? You look familiar." Steve Bird sat smiling and bobbing his head as if keeping time to an invisible band. After hailing me, he'd shifted into automatic pilot.

"Hey, Steve," I addressed him with some vigor; "how about some introductions?"

"Oh, geez, sorry, Bill; uh, that's Crystal," an attractive brunette; "this is Judith," a cute blonde; "and this is Penny," another cute blonde. As I'd thought, they were nurses at St. Luke's, where Steve also worked part-time as an orderly and a blood processor—A, AB, O, negative, positive, that sort of thing. Robertson snagged a chair from a nearby table and sat down next to Crystal. I followed suit and squeezed in between Steve and Judith. We answered the questions that had greeted us. "I'm from Harrisburg; I met Robertson at Dickinson." Dickinson brought forth a trio of O's.

"Actually," Robertson intoned, "I reside right here in Fountain Hill. Perhaps you recognize me because I've been to Pelligatti's frequently in the past three or four years." Another trio of O's.

Robertson, resuming his usual command style, declared, "Ladies and gentlemen, we need another round!"

Judith and Penny, their glasses still half full, declined; they'd have to be leaving soon. Crystal, who didn't need to be hurrying off, would welcome another Chablis.

"And you, Keen and Mr. Bird—beers, I presume?" We nodded. Robertson beckoned the waitress and gave the order, adding a double Cutty Sark on the rocks for him but eyes widened.

Robertson was soon engaged in a one-on-one w ...ystal. Steve and I and the two blondes tossed words back and forth for a while. Then I zeroed in on Judith, discovered that she was not presently entangled with anyone in particular, and got her phone number. She soon announced, "Much as I wish otherwise, I'm going to have to leave—a shift coming up. Coming, Penny?" Penny nodded. Steve and I stood up to clear the way for her; Judith smiled back at me and mouthed, "Call me." I nodded yes. Robertson ordered another round.

Left without ladies to flirt with, Steve Bird and I talked about our plans for the summer. Both of us would be taking Strauch's Carlyle-Arnold seminar. I was staying at the Beta house, I told him. *What about the fall?* he wanted to know. "No plans," I told him. I should consider moving in with him and another intern at the apartment they were renting on Delaware Avenue, close to Pelligatti's and the nurses. I said I'd think about it.

One more round along, Crystal said she needed to call it an evening. She accepted Robertson's offer of a ride. "Wait here, Keen," he commanded; "I shall return anon." I wondered, in Robertson's dictionary, how long was anon? I guess that depended on how free Crystal was with her favors.

Steve Bird and I compared notes on the members of the English Department. He'd been an undergraduate at Lehigh and knew them—which to avoid (there were a few), which were all-around good guys (most of them, indeed, and certainly Ernie Dilworth and Ray Armstrong), and which were must-takes (Professors Severs and Strauch). The processes of the alternative curriculum were alive and well.

Robertson returned sooner than I had expected, entering Pelligatti's on the heels of a flurry of nurses. As he headed toward our booth, his eyes were flashing and there was a bounce in his step. Reading the signs that Robertson was about to launch the bar into an all-night party, I leapt into action. "No, Robertson: don't even think it; you're not buying a round for the whole damn bar."

"Keen, you…"

"Look, Robertson, if you have to party until they close the bar, take me back to campus first. I've got to drive tomorrow."

"Keen, it's only nine…"

"I know what time it is. The hell with it. I'll walk back."

"Oh, Keen, you are stubborn…" Robertson whined as he headed toward the door. I dogged his heels so he wouldn't turn around, called back by the noise, the booze, and the surrounding flesh.

Outside, I stopped and said, "Robertson, I'm sorry I'm being an old stick, but I've got to eat something."

"They sell food at Pelligatti's, Keen."

"So I saw; but ever since we got there, Steve has been drinking on other people's dollars, including several of mine, while you were off with Nurse Crystal. I don't mind buying him a beer; he'd probably do the same for me if I were short of cash. I was afraid if I ordered dinner, I'd have to buy his too; and my reserves are running thin. Man, I need cheap and filling food, and I need it in a hurry."

"Righto, Keen; I know just the place." I'll say this for Robertson; when you got through his enthusiasm for the moment and led him to see your need, he responded fast.

He drove us downhill toward the South Side. Alongside the Wilbur Trust Company, he turned right and pulled over to the curb.

"There it is, Keen—cheap and filling food in a hurry."

I looked over at the shack on the other side. The sign on its lighted window said *Pete's*.

"Pete, the Greek's, Keen: let's eat."

I had heard of Pete the Greek's, the late-night dining choice of bibulous Lehigh boys. I followed Robertson across the street and into the shop. The familiar aroma of grilling dogs, fresh-cut onions, and famous sauce that I'd come to love at The Spot on the square in Harrisburg made me feel right at home. I checked the menu and found fries with gravy: I was golden. "Two with everything, fries with gravy, and a Coke," I said. Robertson ordered six dogs with the works, no fries, no drink. He was a purist. In a second we were served. We stood at the counter and ate the cheap and filling food. Robertson ate in a hurry and had ordered and eaten two more dogs before I finished my original order. "Thanks, Robertson: that was just what I needed."

"Don't be silly, Keen." Robertson's generosity wouldn't take thanks for an answer. Did I mention that he paid for the whole damn thing? As he did, he ordered two more for the road; so we took that wonderful aroma back to the bug and savored it all the way up South Mountain to the Beta house.

In the morning, I gassed up my car, Heap II, at the cheap Esso at the foot of the New Street Bridge and headed home to Harrisburg.

That weekend in Carlisle, I missed the graduates, Hyman and Taylor; but I did spend time with Bob Singdahlsen and Margot Patrick. And, oh, yes, I endured the hostility of the happily married Gretta Zsaban. That hurt a bit, because I had cared for her. I vowed I'd get over it.

CHAPTER THREE

Summertime in the Steel Town: Some New Arrangements

By the middle of June, the Lehigh Valley was suffering a heat wave. On the first morning of Professor Strauch's Carlyle-Arnold seminar, the casement windows of the English seminar room were opened wide to little avail. You'd think a school noted for turning out engineers and captains of industry would be ahead of the game in adopting new technologies. Not to say there were no air-conditioned buildings at Lehigh, but this was the library, the tramping ground of graduate students in the humanities, so, unlike the loftier administrators and scientists, we could sweat it out.

The crew gathered there for instruction included Joe Mooney and Steve Bird, both Lehigh grads and former students of Carl Ferdinand Strauch. The two of them stopped complaining about heat when the great man arrived. They both knew he'd walked from across the river, up into the campus, and up some more to the third floor of the library. If he wasn't bitching about the weather, neither were they. I followed their lead.

Professor Strauch established himself at the head of the table, unloaded a tablet and books from his briefcase, spread them around in front of him like the Maginot Line, surveyed the faces positioned about the table, pointed to the books shelved along the wall to his right, and said, "Those are essential books by and about Thomas Carlyle and Matthew Arnold. Get to know them." We were off and running. The room seemed hotter than ever. Still, no one was complaining.

A couple of days into the course, the heat wave broke, and the course became enjoyable. There were student reports and dynamic readings from Carlyle's prose by Professor Strauch. He enjoyed performing for us passages he called "Carlyle's flame pictures." After the liveliness of those presentations and some memorable discussions of Carlyle's ideas, rhetorical strategies, and structuring devices, Matthew Arnold seemed, to me at least, a bit of a letdown. There were moments, of course, when "a bolt shot back somewhere" in Arnold's lines; but for the most part, his work was wan.

Outside of class, I spent a lot of time with Steve Bird and his roommate, Bob Davies, a veteran back from his service using the GI Bill to take courses at Moravian and, like Steve, working as an orderly at St. Luke's Hospital. I got to see the apartment and thought the kitchen was passable and the living room almost spacious, a good room for parties. I said I'd move in come September. The watering hole of choice that summer was Pelligotti's, where, as often as not, we'd meet off duty nurses. I began to date Nurse Judith. She was a sweet girl who loved music and dancing. I took her dancing at a club over toward Allentown and began to think things were looking up.

Before I knew it, August 22 was about to arrive. From my early school days at Forney, my birthday (you got it, August 22 is my birthday) was a wakeup call to get busy and do summer things because very soon school would be starting up again. I'd promised my parents I'd come home for a week near the end of August. So on August 21, I packed my gear, gassed up the car, called home and told my mother I'd be there for supper, and headed west. Actually, I got there in early afternoon, and brother Jim recruited me for some basketball in Reservoir Park. I'd swear he'd grown six inches since I'd last shot hoops with him, and he was developing some shots.

I suggested we come back one evening when guys were home from work and ready for some games.

Supper was, as usual, a feast. Chicken corn soup! I don't care how hot it is on August 22; it's never too hot for chicken corn soup. And delicious cheeseburgers. I think my mother nixed the cake, but there was definitely Breyers vanilla ice cream. And there were questions galore for the budding college teacher. I fielded ones about the quality of the students, the quality of my professors, and sports. Lehigh had been very good in football, winning the Lambert Cup, and every bit as good in wrestling. What courses would I be taking this year? Chaucer and Donne. Would I be teaching the same one again? Yes, I would. And on and on. Evening basketball at Reservoir would have to be another day. It was too late, and I was too full. Jim and I did make it to the court the next evening. Joe Fiedler was still around, and elder stateman Jack Sutch was still holding down the bench, but most of the other players that evening were closer to Jim's age than mine. I recognized some who, like my brother, had grown like weeds. By this time, everyone got milk at school; still, I wondered what they were fortifying it with to produce such growth. About the time we were calling it quits, a car I thought I recognized pulled up and was being parked near the court. Yep, Ed Schlosser got out of it.

"Hey, Bill; I stopped by your house and your dad said you were down here. I thought you might want to go to the dance at the Y."

"Yeah, Ed; but I need to wash up and change."

"Sure, hop in."

"Hey, Ed, this is my brother Jim." I'd almost said little brother, but then I realized he was taking up as much of the back seat as I was.

"Hi, Jim; you still at Edison?" Ed asked.

"Yeah, one more year."

Pappy was standing at the front door. "Well, Ed, I see you found them," he said.

"Yeah, next time I'll come earlier and join the game."

"Well, come in."

While Pappy and Ed passed the time, I hustled upstairs for a quick washup and change of clothes. Fortunately, the bathroom was unoccupied. I sometimes wondered how the lot of us (seven in summer when Aunt Marion was home) ever made it through all those years with only one bathroom. Now that there's one of me living in a huge house in Arlington, I've got two showers, a tub, and three toilets. Maybe I should take in lodgers.

By the time I was ready, there wasn't going to be much dancing left at the Y. We might get there in time to hear "Goodnight, Sweetheart." Ed was thinking along the same line. "You know, Bill, maybe we ought to just go for beer and pizza."

"Sounds good to me; the basketball wore off my dinner and whomped up a hefty thirst."

"How about Harry's Bar over on Vernon Street? I sometimes run into folks from John Harris there."

"Let's do it."

At Harry's we snagged a table and ordered big frosted goblets of beer and a large pizza with mile-high mushrooms. Our talk turned to "who've you seen" and "what's going on with so-and-so." Since I'd been away most of the summer, Ed did most of the talking. Ed had started at F&M with Fred Castiglia, Don Brauw, and Willie Jones, but after a year, he'd transferred to Juniata, where his dad, Coach Schlosser, had gone to school. Ed had just finished a year of dental school. He said he'd seen Fred and Mike Galdino that summer—right there at Harry's, in fact. He told me he'd been going with a girl at Juniata, but that hadn't worked out. To my question about no dancing at Juniata, he said, "That's a crock. Maybe in the past, but they dance now." That would please my mother.

"You know, don't you, that your old girlfriend Sara Ann has gotten married."

"Yeah, I heard she married a Phi Psi from Dickinson, Anne Gormley's cousin. He was a senior when I first got there. I remember him from rushing, though I didn't join the Phi Psis. Oh, Miles Gibbons did. And do you remember Fred Hamilton, Don Murdoch's friend from western Pennsylvania? He came to that party Peggy Williams invited us to around graduation time. Well, he was a Phi Psi too. It was a good house, a lot of jocks." Our pizza arrived. We ate; we drank the cold beer.

I thought about Sara Ann. She was a really smart young woman. She went to nursing school. "You know, Ed, some of the smartest women at John Harris went to nursing school."

"What brought that up, Bill?"

"Oh, yeah, kind of out of the blue: I was thinking about Sara Ann, a really smart lady who didn't go to college but to nursing school. And Linda, Joanne, Jeannie Hines, and, of course, Carol. They all went to nursing school. Any one of them could have done as well in college as I did. They were all smart enough, and they were downright beautiful."

"Well, Bill, we need nurses, and they'll be good ones."

"You know, Ed, I've been dating a nurse this summer in Bethlehem, a really sweet girl; but she's no Sara Ann, she's no Linda; they were both supersmart. I admired them. Maybe…"

"Maybe what, Bill?"

"Oh, I was just thinking, Sara Ann and Linda, weren't just smart, they were smarter than I was; and I was the one who was going to college." Then something really spooky happened. I looked up and saw, entering Harry's Tavern, one of the nurses I'd just been talking about. It was Carol, Nurse Carol now, the beautiful Carol of our neighborhood who was the chosen girlfriend of superathletes at John Harris.

"Hi, Eddie, hi, Bill," she said, and gave both of us the pleasure of her wonderful smile. The tall guy with her had to be Henning, Nell's brother, the man she was soon to marry. He nodded at us and went off to order.

"It's so good to see both of you. I wish I could stay and talk, but I'm with Pete."

"Hey, another time, Carol," I said. She joined her fiancé.

Several days later, I packed the car and headed back to Bethlehem. It was time to crank things up for the new year.

CHAPTER FOUR

Year Two at Lehigh: Planning for Who-Knows-How-Long

In late afternoon, I arrived at the apartment building on Delaware Avenue where I'd be living with Steve Bird and Bob Davies. Neither of them had done grocery shopping, so I wouldn't be cooking that evening. We headed out to Pelligatti's.

I'd finished my burger and was about to walk back to the apartment when Nurse Judith and two of her friends arrived, so I stayed for one more beer. She said she was glad to see me and asked about my time at home.

I told her about my family and the friends I'd seen. Then the conversation faltered. I sensed she was waiting for me to suggest something, a date, dancing, dinner. But I didn't. I was still thinking about spirits from my past, Sara Ann, Linda, Carol. My atheist friends say I'm a sentimental and superstitious sort. As for Nurse Judith, I knew I'd just be stringing her along, which, I thought, might hurt her more than just breaking it off now. I excused myself, citing work I had to get started on, said good night, and left.

Back at the apartment, I tried to read. It was quiet enough because Steve and Bob were still at Pelligatti's; but I was making no headway, reading the same paragraph three times over and still having no sense of its meaning. I was nearly asleep in the chair when the phone rang. It was Robertson, calling from Pelligatti's, where he had just stopped in and joined Steve and Bob and the nurses. They told him I'd gone back to the apartment. Steve gave him the number.

"No, Robertson, I've been there; and I don't want to go back."

"Nonsense, Keen, you old stick: I'm coming to get you."

I heard the motorcycle screech to a stop on Delaware Avenue. Apparently the flat had been fixed. I heard Robertson thundering up the stairs; he pounded on the door: "Open up, Keen: I've got a warrant for your arrest!"

I opened the door.

"Come, Keen; we must avail ourselves of fast-fleeting time."

"Right, Robertson; but not at Pelligatti's."

"Fine, onward to the Tallyho."

I drank beer; Robertson chose scotch. He was warming up for a full evening of celebration. With Robertson, you didn't ask what the occasion for celebration was, because if there was one, you'd have to listen to its history, and if there wasn't one, he'd invent a preposterous story. I tried to derail the celebration train, because I had to get busy early the next morning. Robertson worked up his best blustering condemnation of my fecklessness, my premature arrival at middle age, and my betrayal of the noble cause of roistering. It was some performance. I wished Hyman and Tsigunos had been there to hear it. So I relented (what the hell, you have to pay the piper something). We had one more drink followed by hotdogs at Pete the Greek's. Finally, Robertson let me go, but not without another lament. "Oh, Keen, how very disappointing you've become!" I walked back to the apartment.

The next morning I set off to find my new office in Christmas-Saucon Hall, greet any friends who were around, and see what other folks had turned up. It was in the English Seminar Room of the library later that morning that I met the new arrival who would change my life. I had climbed the steps up to the third floor and trudged to the room that served as the center of daily life for graduate students in English. Two people had arrived there before me.

"Good googly moo goo, it's Guilliaume, the boy wonder," chortled John Gustavson from the far end of the long seminar table. Gus had started with me as a graduate teaching assistant the year before. He'd done his undergraduate work at Uppsala in New Jersey. At Upsie, he'd met a beautiful blond Swedish American girl named Edie. They'd married just after they graduated. When they'd moved to Bethlehem, Edie had taken a job as a kindergarten teacher in the suburbs. She'd drive Gus to campus early and dump him at the library, where he'd sit on the front steps until it opened at eight. He proclaimed that Lehigh should pay him for guarding the font of all knowledge. Gus had staked out the far end of the seminar table as his personal space, identified by his leather briefcase, his brown lunch bag, and the hugest ashtray in the room. He'd surrounded himself with a stationary front of cigarette and pipe smoke. He coughed a lot, hemmed and hawed, whistled melodies from Beethoven symphonies, and occasionally read a page or two.

At the other end of the table, directly in front of the shelves of reserve books for Professor Severs's Chaucer seminar and as far away from the Gustavson smog as she could get, sat a new student. I took one long look at her and sat down directly across the table, casting my eyes to gaze upon her golden-haired beauty. She probably wasn't Swedish American, but for gaining attention at Lehigh, she was definitely a contender. "Watch out, Edie, you've got competition," I said to myself. This attractive young woman wore a light blue knit sweater adorned with a circle pin. When she stood up to reshelve the volume she'd been reading and pick another, I saw that her outfit was completed by a full plaid skirt, white anklets, and penny loafers. *Miss Ivy League 1958*, I thought. Maybe my fortunes were on the upswing. In any case, I thanked the graduate school deities for enrolling me in the Chaucer seminar and looked forward to seeing more of this lovely young woman each day and on Monday evenings from seven to ten, when the seminar met. I thought perhaps she'd need a doughty knight to escort her to her castle or wherever else she desired to go. If she wasn't already supplied with an entourage, I'd strive to head the line of volunteers.

Returning to her seat and maybe sensing that my gaze was fixed upon her, she looked straight at me with her deep-brown eyes and smiled. That day, for the first of what would become many times, I took her to lunch at the snack bar in the University Center. Did I just say, "I took her to lunch?" Well, actually, maybe you should judge who took whom to lunch. Here is my memory of what occurred.

After fifteen minutes of staring at but not reading a book on Chaucer's narrative technique, I gave up and tried to introduce myself: "Excuse me, miss, I'm…um…I'm…Bill Keen. I'm a second-year English grad student." God, why did I say that? Trying to bolster my courage? Well, it didn't work. Just made me sound like a haughty jerk, a stupid haughty jerk.

But she didn't sneer in the way golden-haired beauties wearing circle pins sometimes do when fumbling oafs address them, and so I stumbled on. "Are you planning to… eat lunch…um…here on campus? If you are, I'd be glad to show you where most of us…um…usually eat lunch, except Gus down there at the other end of the table. He's married… um…and he does the brown bag thing." Why in hell did I say "he's married"? Was I telling her not to waste her time on Gus and look at me? Did I flash my ringless fingers at her? What a jerk I was being! "Oh, maybe I should ask your name, miss." The *miss* routine was sounding stiffer and stupider each time I uttered it.

"Hello, Bill. I'm Sally Whitcomb," she said, adding, "and, yes, I am going to eat here at the University Center, but you don't need to show me around. I already know Lehigh very well. You see, I grew up in Bethlehem," pronouncing the city's name with all its syllables, not *Beth-lum*, the way Pappy did when he talked about his days in the Loop Program.

Sally Whitcomb and I did eat lunch together that day: she did, indeed, know her way around. At noon, we descended the endless stairs to the main floor of the library, strolled through the lobby, and exited through the front door to the parking lot. I followed Sally Whitcomb as she led me up the hillside toward the University Center. It was situated, like a terraced stronghold, on the next level up from the library. Impelled by nerves to break the silence, I blurted out an opening stupidity: "Some hills! Lehigh guys say the local girls have legs like mountain goats." Oh, shit, how to make a good impression.

She laughed and said, "Yes, I've heard that; but I've also heard it doesn't stop Lehigh boys from dating Bethlehem girls." I wondered if she was one who had been squired about by Lehigh boys, but I thought that this wasn't the time to ask.

We finished our climb to the University Center, entered the building, and, detouring around a brace of huge electrified polishers that were constantly buffing the floor of the center, entered the elevator. I pushed the up button and we finally made our way to the snack bar. Sally Whitcomb ordered soup and a salad. The soup was split pea, one of my favorites, so I ordered a bowl and a hot dog. We found a table and sat in silence while we sampled our food. "This is good soup," I said; "I order it whenever they're serving it."

"I haven't had it before, but, you're right, Bill, it is good. It's also served upstairs in the faculty dining room. My father eats there several times a week. He recommended it."

"Your father?"

"Yes, my father, Larry Whitcomb. He's a member of the Geology Department. It's over in Bill Hall. When the weather's nice, he walks over here for lunch. That allows him to catch up on what's going on outside his department."

"Bill Hall? Where's Bill Hall?" It was seeming more and more like I was the beginner.

"Oh, Bill, it's actually Williams Hall, home of the Geology and Biology Departments. The locals call it Bill Hall."

Second-year English grad student? Sally Whitcomb was way ahead of me. I was to learn a lot from her at the snack bar lunches we continued to have on days when she stayed at Lehigh after her morning classes.

Sally had graduated from Pembroke College in Brown University in June 1958. She thought she would be getting married soon after graduation, but her relationship with an older student who'd come back to Brown after military service and begun to date her had fallen apart. She hadn't made other plans. (I knew what that was like, having myself experienced an interruption of expectation.) Sally had come back to Bethlehem and pretty much collapsed in her girlhood bedroom at 431 Washington Avenue. She'd gone out a couple of times with guys she'd known in high school, but mostly she'd stayed in her room and read. (I knew what that was like, too, having used books to dull heartache in my senior year.) We had a lot in common, but I wasn't sure that loss was the best building material for a new relationship.

As summer had neared its end and Sally's father had begun to prepare for the approaching academic year, he's also started to talk to her about what she was going to do. She didn't know. Finally, one evening after dinner dishes had been scrubbed, dried, and put away, he'd said to Sally that, since she could spend all day long in her room reading books, she should put the one thing she liked to do to work by entering the graduate program in English at Lehigh. He'd talked to Professor Severs and made an appointment for her the following morning. "After all, because I'm on the faculty, the fees will be waived; all it will cost me is your lunch money."

You can take the Yankee out of Boston, Larry Whitcomb's hometown, but you can't take practicality out of the Yankee.

Sally had met with Professor Severs. He'd signed her up for the same two seminars I was taking, his Chaucer and Ray Armstrong's Donne. (Thank you, Mother, for taking me to the library and getting me excited about books!) When I could buoy up my conversation with talk about books, I could come off sounding maybe halfway intelligent. Sally and I talked about books—our favorite books, the ones we were reading in class, others we'd come to love in the long years of schooling, and subversive reading in so-called trash that was never included in high school curricula. She was amazed that I listed the Tarzan books and the westerns of Zane Gray among my favorites. Maybe they were guy reads. About poets, we generally agreed—Donne and many of the other seventeenth-century poets, and the Romantics, particularly Keats. T. S. Eliot and Marianne Moore also made both our lists.

In more practical moments, we talked about what we wanted to work at when we finished graduate school and became full-fledged adults. Because of my positive experience in the classroom the year before, I was pretty sure I wanted to be a college teacher. Sally said that until recently, she hadn't thought about teaching. Her father, of course, was a teacher; but making enough to support his family required him not only to do the full-time job at Lehigh but to devote most of the summer to teaching in Penn State's extension program. That had cut into the time he had to do geology fieldwork, slowed down his production of scientific articles, and, she thought, kept him stuck at the associate professor level and led to his first heart attack a few years back.

Sally also said, "Hard as it's been for him, my father loves teaching; and his nudging me into graduate school was to encourage me to become a teacher too." She was almost convinced that her father had put her on the right track. What she said next sealed the deal, for me, at least. "Bill, I know teachers have to scrimp and save; but they also have the summers to travel. I already know how to save, and I'm bound and determined to travel."

Sally spoke from experience about the powerful lure of traveling, seeing all the places she'd read about, visiting the museums and the marketplaces, eating the food, sampling the wine. She'd already been to more places than I had, starting with her summers at the Wavus Camps in Maine and trips to relatives' homes throughout New England. But the grandest experience she'd had was a summer in Europe. Sally had already been to Europe! During the summer between her junior and senior years at Brown, she'd traveled around most of Europe that was then open to students from the United States.

The tour, sponsored by the National Students' Association, started in New York, where the students from many colleges and universities boarded the *Castel Felice*, a troopship that had survived World War II. Across the pond, they were taught how to drive VW bugs and assigned an older European student who spoke several languages as a guide and advisor. Sally's crew of four, all Pembrokers, were directed by Fritz Mueller. Before each day's jaunt, he would tell the group where it needed to get to by dinnertime that day and then show them the options for their day. Sally and her friends, having studied art history at Brown, wished to concentrate on actually seeing the paintings, sculptures, and works of architecture they'd been studying from a distance. In no time, they routinely spent part of each evening mapping out the route to the richest experience of art on the next day. Along the way, they'd visit marketplaces to buy bread and fruit and cheese and other foods that were typical of the region.

When she'd filled me with this story, I let out a cheer that nearly spilled my soup. "You got to travel as freely as that? I want to travel like that! We're going to travel like that. Two teachers can scrimp and save twice as fast as one." I knew as soon as I'd blurted it out that it was a proposal, but I had to spend half a year more to convince Sally that she should accept it.

At first, Sally said to me, "Bill, we're just getting to know one another; let's not rush things."

"Of course not, Sally; we have at least a year to get to know one another better. But I hope that, whenever our studies will set us free for an hour or so a day, we'll make the most of that breathing room together."

"We'll see," Sally said.

We did study together for the two seminars we were both taking. Sally, however, was signed up for a full load of four courses each semester so she could finish the coursework for her MA in one year. I tried to use the time when she was occupied elsewhere and I wasn't teaching to finish as much of my grading and preparation as possible. It was a valuable experience; I frittered away less time than ever before. Sally Whitcomb had given me a focus that I'd never had before, not even when singing in the glee club and working on the Follies and selling sandwiches were controlling my life.

We continued to see one another for lunch most days; and on the weekends there were football games and, later, wrestling matches to go to. Sally was a fan of both sports, particularly wrestling. Having grown up in Bethlehem where, Chuck Bednarik notwithstanding, wrestling is king, Sally knew the sport. She'd been watching from grade school on as Bethlehem boys learned how to grapple, some of them becoming the best in the state; and, of course, as a faculty brat, she'd had ready access to Lehigh's games and matches, as well as its swimming pool and the ROTC firing range, where she became an NRA sharpshooter.

There were also weekend parties on the Lehigh campus— at the Beta house and other fraternities I was being invited to by present and former students. There were occasional faculty parties, quite a few of them at the farmhouse of Ray and Mary Armstrong. We'd drink Ray's home brew and sing the night away. Sally was a strong alto and a wonderful harmonizer. (We were discovering more and more we had in common.) And then there were parties at the Bird-Davies-Keen apartment on Delaware Avenue. It was at one of these parties that Sally got to meet an unforgettable part of my past.

The Christmas season had arrived. A huge Christmas tree rose up at the Y on the Hill to Hill Bridge. Moravian stars began to sparkle on porches. The shops on Main Street were decorated with ribbons and wreaths, and snowflakes, which had held off until then, began to fall and collect in the streets and on the sidewalks and the footpaths at Lehigh. Sally's brother Howard, a sophomore at Brown, came home for the break.

Steve Bird was planning a party for the evening of the final day of classes, the Friday before Christmas. I was to prepare food to balance out the beer and the gin. Most of the folks invited were English graduate students, with a couple from other departments added in, including Ed Smith, a history grad student; Fred Midliddge, in biology; and Earl Knies, a graduate assistant in English—all graduates of Muhlenberg, the nearby liberal arts college that sent loads of its graduates to Lehigh for master's degrees and PhDs. Gus and Edie were there, Gus armed with his oversized ukulele. For Howard

Whitcomb, it was, I believe, the first Lehigh party; surely the first where most of the guests were graduate students. For him, it was bound to be an eye-opener.

By eight o'clock that evening, the living room of our apartment was full of people. All the chairs, the couch, and the window seats were occupied. In the middle of the living room the table sat loaded with nibblies, easy stuff you could pour out of bags and cans—potato chips and pretzels and mixed nuts. Also, I'd made a dip out of sour cream, Lipton soup, and clams. It was a hit, so the table got a lot of standing-room-only traffic. Edie had brought Christmas cookies. The drinks were in the kitchen, where the thirstiest partiers had squeezed in. Gus had his ukulele going, and the kitchen-dwellers soon began to try out their voices.

By eleven o'clock the nibblies were about gone. It looked like someone had licked the bowl that had contained the dip. The voices in the kitchen were getting louder and increasingly off-key. Steve Bird, ordinarily a baritone, had become a screaming first tenor (would he be hoarse in the morning!). With all this racket, I hadn't heard the late arrival coming up the stairs until he burst through the door. "Oh, Keen, you ingrate, why wasn't I invited to this party?" Robertson boomed.

"R. Blaylock, I didn't know you were home. You never get in touch in advance; you just show up like an unannounced tidal wave."

"A what., Keen?"

"Come on in, Robertson; there's beer in the kitchen, and, oh, yeah, gin, if you'd prefer. See if you can push your way through the choir and serve yourself."

"Of course, I'd prefer gin: and, as a former gridiron great at Dear Old Dickinson, I'll reach the goal line where the gin sits."

Apparently he scored and had been recruited by the choristers, because soon I heard him enriching the singing with his powerful bass voice as they delivered a very loud rendition of "Old Man River," followed by Robertson's usual solo, "My Father Killed a Kangeroo." Some of the guests began to leave. There are timid souls everywhere.

There was a break in the singing. Robertson stormed from the kitchen, surged into the living room, and leapt up onto a now-vacant spot on a window seat while holding a drink in one hand and grabbing a pillow with the other. I won't say he didn't spill a drop, but he ended standing upright and facing into the room (how the hell did he do that?), the pillow perched atop his head. Like a searchlight, he scanned the faces of the remaining guests, smiled, and began to recite,

Terence, this is stupid stuff:
You eat your victuals fast enough:
There can't be much amiss, 'tis clear,
To see the rate you drink your beer.

Robertson forged on without a skip up to "And down in lovely muck I've lain,/Happy til I woke again," at which point he hopped down from his perch, bowed, saluted the remaining guests, and quaffed his beverage. I was reminded of his recitation outside of Carlisle to a field full of cows, but this audience didn't moo: it cheered and applauded.

Then the big fellow turned to me and said, "Keen, who are these fine people?"

Sally was right beside me. I took her hand, turned to Robertson and said, "This is Sally Whitcomb."

"I see," he said. "Sally Whitcomb, I've heard of you, the young lady who is keeping the company of William P. Keen, the famous sandwich man."

"Well, Mr. Taylor, I am dating Bill: but I don't know anything about a sandwich man."

"Well," Robertson replied, "that's a story you must eventually hear." Addressing Howard, who was standing next to his sister and staring wide-eyed at the big wind that had just blown in, Robertson inquired, "And who are you, my fine young fellow?"

Howard was temporarily speechless, so Sally answered, "That's my brother Howard; he's home from Brown for Christmas."

"Well, it's certainly good to meet you, my boy."

Remembering Robertson's power over Hyman, Tsigounis, and myself, I thought the big guy had just recruited another follower.

At that point, John Gustavson emerged from the kitchen, strumming his ukulele and singing,

O, the Ir-rye-e is arisin'

and the beer is a-getting' low.

"Zounds," said Robertson; "and we have more songs to sing and tales to tell. A further supply of beer is required. Off to Pelligatti's before it's too late." Turning to Howard, he said, "Come, Sancho Panza, my steed awaits," and led Howard out of the room and down the stairs.

I said to Sally, "We may never see your brother alive again."

She rolled her eyes. But I was wrong. Ten minutes later, Robertson thundered back into the room, Howard following him, toting a bag of quarts. How they and the beer managed to get back undamaged on Robertson's motorcycle remains a mystery.

On Christmas Day, I was invited to dinner at the Whitcombs'. I spent most of the time before dinner getting to know Howard better. As a sophomore, he was already a starter on Brown's soccer team. He'd pledged Delta Tau Delta, whose membership included lots of athletes. He was majoring in political science and, at that moment, at least, was interested in Barry Goldwater, whose *Conscience of a Conservative* he was reading over the Christmas vacation. I knew that Ruth and Larry Whitcomb would approve of their son's choice; so I kept my attitudes to myself, as did Sally, who, like me, was leaning toward the liberal.

The following day, Sally and I took the train to Harrisburg to visit my family. Sally would be meeting them for the first time. We rode the Reading Railway, dubbed by inveterate travelers forced to use it the "square wheel line." I'd phoned Pappy, who said he'd pick us up at the station. When we arrived in Harrisburg, there wasn't much of a crowd waiting for the train, so I saw my father right away and, pointing him out to Sally, said, "There's my father." Then I saw that my mother was there too. I hadn't expected her. I probably should have guessed she'd come with Pappy, because she seldom missed the opportunity to go for a ride. I started to say, "And, oh, there's…"

"That beautiful woman is your mother?" Sally exclaimed. "She doesn't look old enough to be your mother!"

I did the math fast (I *can* add and subtract): "She's fifty-two." At that age, my mother was still a natural brunette who looked years younger than she was. From Sally's reaction, I wondered if my mother's looking so young was a problem. If it was, she kept it to herself. Still, I sensed I needed to let Sally know how beautiful I thought Sally Whitcomb was, not as if I were a Petrarchan sonneteer exuding hyperbole but with more delicacy and humor. I hoped I was capable. I didn't want to lose her; and I still wasn't sure I'd earned from her an affection with the strength to last. Maybe I shouldn't have worried so much, because the blend of friendliness, enthusiasm, and sophistication that was natural to her won my family's approval. Pappy was wowed by her, as I thought he would be; Aunt Marion, I could see, approved of her manners; sister Barbie immediately adopted Sally as the sister she had always wanted. Brother Jim, I think, appreciated the sincerity with which she listened to him. My mother, well, she always was hard to read. She listened attentively, smiled frequently, gave little nods of agreement, but didn't say much. I hoped she approved of my choice. I hoped she was happy I'd found Sally. But most of all, I hoped Sally would be happy I'd found her. And of that, I was still not sure.

We returned to Bethlehem on December 29, because we'd been invited to a New Year's Eve party at the home of Steve Bird's parents in a rural neighborhood west of Bethlehem near Allentown. We were running a tad late, so when we arrived, we discovered their large backyard almost filled with parked cars. I managed to find a spot and squeeze into it. "Looks like a huge crowd," I said.

"Bill, let's not go in right away," Sally suggested. Eager as I was to join the festivities, I relaxed and sat back in my seat.

"Yes, Bill, I'd be happy to marry you…in two and a half years."

"Oh, Sally, thank you, but why so long a wait?"

"We both have one more semester at Lehigh; and you should go on for a PhD. I'll be spending the next weeks writing to prep schools who are looking for young women to teach upper-school English. I need to prove something for myself and repay my parents for my trip to Europe. I'll be looking for a position that will give me two years. When I've taught for two years, I'll be glad to marry you." When Sally had decided on a course of action, she organized her thoughts and delivered them without a hitch. I admired her ability. I actually learned from her how to overcome my own uncertainty as a speaker. Two and a half years was a long time, but I resolved to follow her lead and begin to search for a program to continue my education.

By the end of April 1959, Sally had done her search and had accepted a position teaching upper-school English at Emma Willard in Troy, New York. For my part, I had asked Professor Severs if he would recommend programs where I might work toward a PhD. He said that he would and that he'd be glad to write letters in support of my applications. The schools he suggested I apply to were Florida State, Syracuse, and LSU. They were all solid graduate schools with established programs in Middle English literature, a field I was interested in, and he had working relationships with the Chaucerians at all three. I accepted his advice.

Several weeks later, I received an offer from Professor Kirby, expert in Middle English language and literature and chairman of English at LSU. It was to study there and to again teach freshman English. I accepted. For the next two years, I was going to be writing lots of letters to stay in touch with the woman I intended to marry. Several weeks later, the fates that play with people's lives sent me a similar offer from

Syracuse University, an easy traveling distance from Troy, New York. I cursed the bad timing, but I had given my word, and I was going to keep it. I'd be writing lots of letters. What else I'd be doing there will have to wait for another time.

CHAPTER FIVE

A Wedding in Bethlehem:
Living with Change

On Saturday, July 15, 1961, Sally and I were married at Trinity Episcopal Church in Bethlehem. There had been a mighty late-morning downpour, and my family had arrived just in time. Pappy had waited out the worst of the storm underneath one of the bridges he'd designed.

In September, I started my first full-time teaching job back at Lehigh. I'd been offered and had accepted a two-year instructorship while, supposedly, I would pass my general exams and language exams in French and German and make a healthy start on my dissertation. Then, as Professor Severs explained his thinking, degree in hand, I would find a job at some other school and wow the people there with my prowess and the high quality of teacher and scholar turned out by that very small graduate program in Bethlehem. I wonder if Professor Severs hadn't heard of the ABD (All But Dissertation), the level at which most candidates were stuck when they searched for the first big job away from the mother ship.

Sally, with two years of successful teaching at Emma Willard to her credit, had no trouble finding a position at William Allen High School in Allentown, despite having not one credit of the required education courses. The principal of William Allen sensed a bargain and offered her a salary lower than she should have accepted, but she did accept it, convincing me she should because we could live on my Lehigh salary and bank all of hers: "Bill," she said, "that's a lot of gravy."

First change in plans: I was awarded a fellowship meant to speed up the completion of my work by freeing me from teaching. The fellowship would pay about a third as much as my salary. We'd have to live on Sally's salary and try to bank mine, a lot less gravy.

Second change in plans: Sally said "No!" when she was offered a second year at William Allen. Why? Isn't a bird in the hand...forget the cliché. To keep the job, she'd have to start taking education courses at Lehigh, a chore that would continue summer after summer until she'd completed thirty hours. "Bill, I've been mentored by master teachers at Emma Willard; I don't need thirty hours of education courses in a department that many professors at Lehigh frown upon. If I go to Lehigh every summer, I'm taking English courses until I've had everything they offer." Then, the straw that broke... again, forget it. When she asked for a room of her own (Sally had read Virginia) instead of having to cart around more than an armload of books and other teaching aids among four different rooms, they had said, "No!" By the end of the week she had lined up a job at the Great Valley Girl Scouts Council in Allentown. Third change in plans: biology screamed, "Hurry up, please; it's time." Before Sally had worked day one for the Girl Scouts, she had to call Libby Figner, the head of the council, and offer to resign because she was expecting a baby in April. As Sally reported the leader's response to me, it was that the council always got good work out of pregnant employees: a ripening (married) young woman was a wholesome influence on the young girls she would meet in visiting various troops, and she could work as long as she and her doctor thought she was able, take a maternity leave, and return to finish up her year by the end of the summer. That was that.

Fourth change in plans: you've already guessed, haven't you? On April 10, 1963, Suzanne Parker Keen was born. Sally rested and recuperated for two weeks. I, having had a much younger brother, showed her how to change a diaper. Sally went back to work, and I became Suzanne's nursemaid, while I continued to study and to search for a job.

IV

JUST KEEP ON DIGGING

CHAPTER ONE

Oswego and Dempster: Shoveling Snow

Fifth change in plans: after a search of local schools turned up nothing, I flung the net further and finally caught a fish along the southern shore of Lake Ontario. Sally and I and Suzanne would be moving to Oswego, New York. I'd be teaching at Oswego State College. Since transitions usually cause delays, we figured we'd be waiting an additional year for our big trip.

Believe me, there were complications and delays. Every year, from Thanksgiving past Easter, even when the moveable feast occurred late in April, I shoveled snow and read endless student papers. This was before the age of part-time staff (adjuncts); the newly-hired full-timers were the adjuncts. There may have been some small classes at Oswego, but I never saw one. The administration was filling up the dorms and overloading freshman comp and sophomore lit. By the end of our first year at Oswego, I'd finished only one chapter of my dissertation.

Sixth change in plans: all the snow-shoveling must have built up my appetites. On April 10, 1965, Rebecca Newell Keen was born, two years and one minute after the birth of her sister Suzanne. The pace of propagation was certainly running on a regular schedule. I taught summer school and did very little on my dissertation.

One step forward: in September 1965, I returned to Lehigh and retook the oral part of my general examination and passed it with ease. The first time around, I'd passed the written exam in one full day of writing about everything from Beowulf to Virginia Woolf; but on the following afternoon, so tired I could hardly remember my own name, I had failed the oral.

"The Winter Wonderland: An Interlude"

It was August 1965. There were four of us now. I had recently finished teaching two summer courses at Oswego. Sally and I and the girls were living in Dempster, New York, a country neighborhood about a mile outside the village of New Haven. In Dempster, there were ten or so houses, a grange hall, a field full of empty fifty-five gallon barrels, lots of cows, and a sawmill. We did have indoor plumbing, a telephone, and, most of the time, electricity. Calls to Niagara Mohawk about our erratic service proved fruitless. Our neighbor, Art Holliday, warned us that the furnace motor could be damaged if it switched on while we were operating on low voltage, the problem caused by our faulty connection. But it was summer: we weren't using the furnace. We made ritual calls to the electric company and hoped the problem would be solved before the weather turned cold.

Sally, who, while I taught, had been isolated all day long with two little girls, and then further isolated for two summer months, needed a break: "Bill, we have to get out of here." It wasn't merely a statement; it was a statement with oak-leaf clusters! I had just received my summer school pay, so I couldn't plead poverty. Sally's parents were in Maine. My parents rarely went anywhere. So we called them. "Come on down," Pappy declared.

So we went to Harrisburg, giving Pappy and my mother a chance to practice being grandparents to Suzanne and Rebecca. We stayed for three days and spent an evening with Bill Greenawalt and his wife Bobbi. They were living at Bill's boyhood house on Nineteenth Street. The next day, we drove to Carlisle and visited with Heber Harper. Then we plopped the girls down on the Dickinson campus near Old West and Bosler Hall and were about to have a very rudimentary picnic lunch when Don Flaherty came by. After introductions, he led us in a flock to his nearby apartment for a feed. There were good shepherds at Dickinson.

When it was time to think about getting back to Oswego, Sally said, "Bill, let's go Route 22 back by Bethlehem: it's not that far out of the way. We can stay at Washington Avenue. My parents aren't there, but I have a key to the house." That's what we did. Arriving just after lunch, we visited briefly with Henny and Walter Fleck, the Whitcombs' closest neighborhood friends and Sally's honorary aunt and uncle.

Later that afternoon, on a chance, I called Robertson's home and reached his father, who told me Robertson and his wife Joan were living in a reconverted mill just outside of

Bethlehem. I called the number he gave me and invited them for a drink, etc., etc. "We'll be there momentarily, Keen," R. Blaylock replied.

About an hour later, the Taylors arrived. We sat in the backyard and drank G&Ts and caught up on the news. Joan Taylor had followed Sally as a professional worker for the Girl Scouts, a job Sally had led her toward during our last summer in Bethlehem. Robertson quizzed me about Oswego. "The students couldn't be as good as Dickinson's," he proclaimed.

"Hard to tell, Robertson, but because two-thirds of them are women, more work gets done by them than ever did by you and me."

"Hmm, yes, that's probably true," he admitted; then, changing the subject, he asked, "What about the weather?"

"Well, it's dry most of the summer; but from Thanksgiving on, even into May, it snows."

"Snow, Keen, that's the stuff! I want to see some snow. Joan," he added, turning to his wife, "we will be visiting William Parker and Sarah Lowell in Oswego next winter."

Joan rolled her eyes.

Oswego's first-semester finals ended just after the middle of January, but my work wouldn't be finished for several days because, by the bad luck of the draw, I had had two late exams in large sophomore literature courses. The exams were all essays. I would be reading the students' work and figuring out final grades for most of the break between semesters.

Sally had been wanting to go home for a visit. Neither of her parents being in the best of health, she wanted to see them and let them get to know their granddaughters. She'd left the day before my last exams. Having nothing scheduled for that day, I'd driven her, Suzanne, and Rebecca to the bus station in Syracuse. Without interruptions, I'd made decent time grading the papers, reviewing each student's work, and assigning final grades.

On the morning of January 24, I drove into Oswego to turn in my grades. The area had had some snow, about eighteen inches in the last week: but the plows had kept up with it and the roads were in good shape with only an inch or so of hard-packed snow that was actually an aid to the driver. At the English Department office, I ran into two of my buddies, Hugo Theimer and Jim Zipinski. We went to lunch together at the reconverted Howard Johnson on the main drag.

As I drove back to Dempster in midafternoon, occasional flakes were falling on my windshield. Nothing to worry about: it would hardly add to the accumulation. After supper that evening I phoned Sally in Bethlehem to see how things were going and check on her plans for coming home, since I'd have to drive to the bus station to collect her and the girls.

"Oh, Bill, you won't have to come to Syracuse to get us: Robertson and Joan are coming for a visit; they'll bring us home. It'll be a tight fit in that VW, but we're all troopers." Yes, they were all troopers; I was sure they would manage.

On January 27, the snow started early in the morning before I was awake. When I rolled over and was brought to full awareness by the gray morning light, I could see heavy snow falling outside my bedroom window. Downstairs, while I waited for the coffee to brew, I listened for the weather report. Heavy snow was falling all along the southern shore of Lake Ontario, and Oswego was getting the worst of it. The prediction was that the blizzard wasn't going to stop anytime soon. From what the broadcaster said, this storm had been expected, and the station had been predicting it for several days. I'd been buried in exams, not listening to the radio. It sounded as if I'd dug out from under the exams and was about to be buried in snow.

I tried to call Sally but with no luck. We were on a multiple-party line; every time I tried, the line was busy. It was already evening by the time I reached her. She said she'd heard there wasn't much accumulation south of Syracuse, and she was confident the Oswego plows would handle the job up there. "Besides," she added, "Robertson is as excited as a kid on Christmas Eve; you tell us not to come and you'll never hear the end of it." That was certainly true.

On Friday, the plows ran regularly from New Haven down toward the sawmill, the site of frequent fires. That road never closed. I began to shovel. Starting at the mouth of our driveway, I tried to shovel my way back to the edge of the porch, about fifteen yards. The snow was coming down so fast that

I was moving backwards. Finally, I settled on trying to clear a spot large enough to hold a VW and a path wide enough for people to get from the car to the porch. Keeping that spot clear and that path open took hourly efforts all day long.

It was eight o'clock and dark as it gets. I was at the mouth of the driveway removing the last hour's accumulation when I recognized headlights, dimmed by the falling snow, but, by damn, a car's headlights; not a plow's, a car's. Then I heard the unmistakable clattering of a VW.

When Robertson's black VW turned into the spot I'd kept clear, I had to lean back into a seven-foot snowbank to avoid being run over. Robertson hopped out the driver's side. "William P. Keen, could you not have made this parking place a bit wider?"

"Good grief, Robertson: I've been shoveling all day long just to keep this much clear. But where is Sally? Where are my girls?"

"They're in the back seat. Joan will have to disembark so that they can struggle their way out. Well, William, this is quite some snowstorm!"

"Yeah, when you say you want to see some snow, Oswego comes through."

Suzanne bounced out of the back, bundled like an Eskimo: "Daddy. Daddy, we're home!" She embraced me around the knees, knocking me further back into the snowbank. And then there was Sally in her Harris Tweed and her Russian hat; and in her arms, wrapped in an heirloom bunting, was Rebecca. We squeezed through the channel I'd dug up to the porch and went inside.

"Wonderful. It's warm in here," said Joan. "That VW heater is for the birds."

"Yeah, I've had the furnace roaring all day because, every hour, I've had to shovel snow; and I've come back in feeling like a popsicle."

As if reading my mind and sticking their tongues out at me, the lights flickered, then went out. For a count of ten, we were in the dark. Then the lights went on again but continued to flicker. Sally ran to the kitchen for candles and matches. We placed candles at strategic points around the first floor. "How romantic," Joan Taylor said: "A candlelit supper." Actually, the lights stayed on, but they flickered a lot. I went to the basement and turned off the furnace. Back upstairs, I advised my guests, "Enjoy the heat while it lasts: I just turned off the furnace."

"Why, Keen, why turn off the furnace?" Robertson demanded.

"Because low voltage could damage the motor."

"How long until we begin to freeze to death, William?"

"We won't freeze. I turned the oven on. It'll work and won't be damaged; but pretty soon, the only warm place will be the kitchen." The kitchen was just large enough to squeeze in a card table and four chairs.

"What about the fridge and the freezer? They've got motors—will they be damaged?" Sally asked. I wasn't sure, so I pulled their plugs. We put the beer and the ice trays in the utility room; it was always cold. We opened the fridge and freezer only when we absolutely needed to, hoping that the food wouldn't spoil. I thought the freezer would be OK. It was filled with packages of frozen beef, half a steer's worth, better than ice cubes. While Sally made supper—pork and sauerkraut—the rest of us sat in the cooling living room, covered by blankets.

After we'd eaten the pork and sauerkraut and binged on ice cream which, if not eaten, would have melted, Sally and I shooed the others back out of the kitchen and did a quick wash of the dishes. Then, at her suggestion, I brought in Monopoly. We listened to the radio and collected rents. It was almost like an adventure. When it was time for bed, Suzanne slept with Robertson and Joan, Rebecca with Sally and me.

The next day, snow continued to fall. Robertson and I shoveled it, Robertson singing "Yo-ho-ho, and a bottle of rum." Just as we'd finished digging out the VW, a butterfly snowplow rumbled past and filled the space we'd cleared. We retreated to the house and downed shots—against heart attacks. On Sunday, the Linns, our faculty friends who lived on the same road but up in New Haven, called to see how we were. Sally told them about the low voltage and the cramped kitchen. The Linns, who had full power, invited us to join them in their warm house. Robertson and I surveyed the situation in the driveway. The VW was a seven-foot-tall white lump. We heard the rumbling of a butterfly snowplow and retreated to the porch.

The VW was an eight-foot-tall white lump. We started to dig. It took an hour. By the time the VW was cleared of snow and fired up, Sally and Joan and the girls were suited up and ready to go. Sally had done a quick raid of the freezer and snagged a standing rib roast. We'd have taken beer and booze too, but there wasn't room.

What a party! Most of the afternoon, Suzanne and the younger Linn kids, Holly and Heather, played in a vacant room in the rambling farmhouse. Sally, Nancy Linn, and Nancy's daughter Jenny and son Jeff played Monopoly. Chuck Linn, Joan, Robertson, and I played bridge. Rebecca slept a bit and got passed around for snuggles with the Linn girls. At cocktail hour, Chuck broke out a bottle of Old Tennis Shoe and made Manhattans. Then we feasted on rare standing rib and roast potatoes. After a long digestion-fostering coffee session, we began to sing, Nancy Linn pounding the piano while the rest of us belted out "The Lost Chord" and "The Holy City" and, oh, of course, "Old Man River," followed by Robertson's solo work on "My Father Killed a Kangeroo."

Robertson and Joan had intended to drive back to Bethlehem on Monday, but that was a no-go. Butterfly plows kept the road from the fire station to the sawmill open for all the days of the storm. Points for the locals. It took until Wednesday morning for county and state plows to open US 104 and 11. Points for them too. I-81 wouldn't be freed up and drivable for another week. Points there? Are you kidding me? Robertson and Joan left on Wednesday, knowing it would be a long trip down Route 11 and hoping that all the little towns they'd be driving through had butterfly snowplows as efficient as ours.

After that storm and Niagara Mohawk's repairing the connection of our power line, I experienced a great relief and, eventually, even felt good about the experience: we'd gotten through it, and we'd had a wonderful day with the Linns'. Best of all, Robertson had had his eyes opened to a force bigger than he. I knew he'd never forget Oswego's big snow; we'd be talking about it for years to come. Still, I wondered how many more superstorms I was capable of surviving. I began to think about moving. Because of Oswego's heavy workload and my ever-increasing responsibilities as a husband and father, I wasn't making much headway on my dissertation: Harry Bailly and the pilgrims were stalled just outside the Tabard at the Watering of St. Thomas. I sat in my office and wondered if I'd ever dig my way out from under all the freshman comp and sophomore lit papers.

Then, before the great white time-consumer had melted, Erwin Palmer and the other power brokers in the English

Department had ramped up a push to develop a PhD program. By March, they were beginning to hire associate professors, folks who'd finished their dissertations, and creative writers, who didn't need to. These new faculty weren't going to reduce the numbers in the labor-intensive courses Hugo Theimer, Jim Zapinski, and I would continue to teach.

On the day I heard we'd just hired two more creative writers and a third medievalist, bumping me from second to third in line for the Chaucer course, I drove home in a reflective funk. Sally knew there was a problem as soon as I entered the house and brushed off Suzanne, who was running at me for a hug. "What's wrong, Bill? It's not like you to ignore Suzanne."

"Get out the typewriter, honey; we've got to find another job. This afternoon I told Erwin Palmer I won't be back next September. We're heading south."

The look she gave me was as threatening as the weather had been. It took me a bourbon old-fashioned and a back rub to get her on board. Even then, there were conditions. I didn't just have to find a job. I'd have to find one at a school and in a place she'd agree to. And that requirement would begin when we started to make our list. One more time— when *we* started to make the list. Fair enough, I guess. Sally took the lead: "What kind of school, Bill?"

"A liberal arts college, Sally."

"What kind of location, Bill?"

"Near or in a big city, Sally."

"How big a city, Bill?"

"At least as big as Bethlehem, Sally."

"Not big enough, Bill."

"But with Allentown and Easton thrown in, that's pretty big, Sally."

"Hmm. Give me some examples, Bill."

"Dickinson, Sally."

"What big city is near Carlisle, Bill?"

"Harrisburg, Sally."

"No!"

"Washington DC and Philadelphia, Sally."

"Neither is near enough. We're closer to Syracuse right now, and we hardly ever get there."

"But it doesn't snow as much in Pennsylvania, Sally."

"Hmm. OK, that's one, Bill."

"Muhlenburg, Sally."

"Two."

"Union, Sally, and maybe you could teach at Emma Willard."

"Yes, that's possible, Bill. Three."

"Gettysburg, Sally, closer to DC than Dickinson is."

"Four."

"Allegheny, an hour from Pittsburgh, Sally."

"Well, OK. But, you know, it does snow north of Pittsburgh."

That's the way it went until we had listed ten schools. Sally said, "Since I'll be typing the letters, I'll need another back rub, Bill."

"And another old-fashioned, Sal babes?"

"Why not, Bill."

A couple of days later, I got a phone call from my friend Ed Smith, who was in the History Department at Buffalo State. I told him our plan, and Smith nearly leapt through the phone: "Keen, there are two or three jobs at W&J. It's closer to Pittsburgh than Allegheny is." That made eleven, one of my lucky numbers.

Sally typed. I made old-fashioneds and administered back rubs. From those eleven unsolicited letters, I got two interviews and one new job.

CHAPTER TWO

Washington and Jefferson College: September 1966 to June 1972

I started at W&J as an assistant professor who would still be teaching freshman comp. That didn't bother me. I'd learned at Lehigh and LSU that freshman comp was the bread-and-butter course. I expected to teach it for most of my career. The positive difference was that W&J limited the size of freshman sections to fifteen students. During my first year, I'd be teaching three sections, a total of forty-five students, five fewer than I'd had in two sections at Oswego. And I soon found that W&J's students were better prepared and, by and large, more highly motivated than the students at Oswego. W&J guys wanted to be doctors and lawyers and knew they had to work hard to enter the schools leading to those professions.

The freshman classes I'd be teaching met on Tuesday, Thursday, and Saturday mornings at eight, nine, and eleven.

My third course, a seminar in Joyce and Yeats, met once a week, on Monday afternoon from one to four. I scheduled my office hours for Monday morning and Tuesday and Thursday afternoons. That gave me all day Wednesday and all day Friday to work on my dissertation. During that school year and the following summer, I finished the job. I would be receiving my degree on Founder's Day in October.

Sally was pregnant, but this time we weren't expecting an April baby. Late October had been penciled in for the arrival of Sam/Rachel; we knew the names but not the gender. I'd have to fly to Bethlehem on the seventh of October to receive my degree the following day. Sadly, I'd be flying alone, because Sally's doctor said she should not fly. She was disappointed; after all that time supporting me, she wouldn't see me walk across the stage. But a healthy baby was the highest priority for both of us.

Who did make it? Sally's parents were there, as were mine: and Heber Harper had ridden with them to Bethlehem. They knew how much I owed him. During the long years when I thought the process would never end and I felt like quitting, Heber would say, "No, Bill, don't end up like me; finish your dissertation!" I'd listened.

After the ceremony, Pappy drove us across the New Street Bridge to Church Street, where Robertson and Joan were living. They were hosting a party for me. The Whitcombs were there, and my old professors, Ray Armstrong and

Ernie Dilworth. We drank dry sherry and ate little sandwiches (no hot dogs from Pete the Greek's). Robertson
made a speech about the famous sandwich man becoming a
PhD, a process which somehow involved a caterpillar and a
butterfly. We called Sally, and all who knew her took a turn
on the phone, Robertson chiding her for getting pregnant
and missing his party.

At the Pittsburgh airport I was met by my beautiful wife
and my two wonderful little girls. It was a time when people
meeting planes could still go out on the tarmac—no big-deal
security then. Suzanne and Rebecca mobbed me with hugs.
Sally freed me from their affectionate grappling, leaned over
the best she could, and said to them, "What do you say to
your father?"

"Congratulations, Dr. Keen!" they squealed.

"Thank you, Suzy; thank you, Becca."

"Now, can we stop calling him Dr. Keen?" Rebecca asked,
arms akimbo, right foot tapping to the rhythm of her words.

Sally laughed: "Of course, girls, from now on, he's Daddy
or just plain Bill."

Two weeks later, Rachel arrived, October 23, 1967. Soon
after mother and daughter came home from the hospital,
Sally and I began to discuss the big trip—when, for how
long, and where specifically. "Not next summer or the summer after that, either, Bill: We should wait until Rachel can
keep up and all three girls can follow directions. Besides, why

go for only a summer? If we wait until you're eligible for a sabbatical, we can go for a whole year!"

"I have to get tenure first: then in my sixth year I can apply for a sabbatical in the seventh; that would make it the summer of 1972. Rachel will certainly be able to walk by then. As for following directions…"

"Oh, stop it, Bill: they're girls. Girls follow directions!"

I bought Sally's argument. If the girls had been teenagers…well, I don't know. But they'd be nine, seven, and four and a half—maybe it would work.

So that was the plan: summer of 1972, for a year. Check that—for fifteen months. I thought I'd better publish something to shore up my case for tenure. W&J prided itself on being a teachers' school, where lack of publication didn't necessarily mean you'd perish; but I knew that the full professors on the tenure committee had published articles and books. An article or two wouldn't hurt my chances. Walter Sanderlin, a full professor in history and a member of the tenure committee, had been on my back to submit an article to *Topic,* W&J's own journal for special studies in the liberal arts. Time to get Harry Bailly ready to lead us to Canterbury. Walter Sanderlin liked my piece on Chaucer's Host, selecting it to be the lead article in the Spring 1969 issue of *Topic.* I breathed a little easier. When tenure came my way the following year, Sally said, "Now, Bill, let's plan the trip!"

We checked our savings and figured how much more we could save by the time we could go, assuming I'd be awarded a sabbatical.

Next question: where should we go? I suggested Ireland in general and Dublin in particular because of my interest in Yeats and Joyce, which had become my "area" because Chaucer was owned by a senior professor. I was teaching only "The General Prologue" and a few of the tales in the sophomore-level survey course.

Sally vetoed Ireland and Dublin.

"What's wrong with Dublin, Sal?"

"Nothing, and we can go there for a week or so from England; but from what I've been reading, the state schools are not good, and we can't afford to put the girls in a private school. In England, the state-run schools are better."

"So, where in England, Sal?"

"Not London, but in a good-sized city close to London, because the best way to travel in England is by train; and to do that, we'll have to go to London first. I think we should live in Oxford or Reading…wait a minute…Cambridge. We should live in Cambridge. You'd have access to a great library, Cambridge is big enough to have its own cultural life, and it's an easy trip to London by train; and besides, we have friends in Cambridge."

"What friends?"

"John and Shiela Gatiss."

John and Shiela Gatiss had lived a couple of doors down Beau Street when we first moved to Washington. I remembered that John, an engineer who'd worked at Drankenfeld, had graduated from Cambridge; but I also recalled that he was from London. So I raised the point.

Sally parried my thrust: "Yes, John was from London originally, but when they decided to go back to England last year, the Gatisses chose to live in Cambridge. Shiela says the state-run schools in Cambridge are far superior to any schools in Ireland. Besides, she's promised to find a place for us near them, so we won't have to do a search in a strange town while we're jet-lagged from our flight."

The low-watt bulb in my brain finally twinkled on. Sally already knew where we were going to live, and she could read my mind.

"And T. R. Henn, the Yeats scholar you so admire, still lives in Cambridge."

Damn straight; Sal could read my mind. Her wizardly ancestors back in Salem would be proud of her—with the possible exception of Samuel Sewell. So, if or when I received news of my sabbatical, we would be heading to Cambridge and taking side trips to wherever my life planner decided we should go. And that was fine with me, as long as I didn't have to paddle a canoe.

CHAPTER THREE

Flying to Cambridge: June 1972

Early in the spring of 1972, I received a letter from the President's Office informing me that I had been awarded a sabbatical for the following academic year. Sally and I celebrated and began to whip up enthusiasm in our three daughters. I wasn't surprised that we met some resistance. After all, we'd be taking them away from their familiar world for nearly fifteen months—a large chunk of life for even the oldest. Suzanne would miss her school friends; Becky would miss our two cats as well as her school friends; and though Rachel may not have known who she would miss, she wasn't going to be left out of the sisterly resistance.

Sally did a good job on them, recreating from her own experience the thrill of travel and raiding Citizens Library for books full of enticing pictures. We promised to rent our house to people who loved cats and who would take good care of Andy and Geoff. We made a big deal out of taking preparatory trips to the Pittsburgh airport, where we would watch planes arrive and depart while keeping a sharp eye for happy passengers whose dreams had been fulfilled or were brimming with expectation about what lay ahead. And as the time of departure grew near, we put them through the airport drill. Sally had made an airport uniform for the girls— brightly striped pants with hippy-flared bell-bottoms. We instructed the girls to hold hands and try to keep up with us as we charged through the corridors. The competitive trio rose to the bait and stuck right on our tails.

As the time for us to fly grew closer, we had to channel the girls' building excitement by making lists and compiling necessities, tactics which often added to the tension: "Where's my Woolrich jacket, Sal?"

"Wherever you put it; it doesn't fit me."

"Why'd you put my dress shoes on the list, Sal?"

"For the *France*; you'll need them for the *France*—and the dark suit too."

"The *France*?"

"Yes, the *France*; I'm coming home on the *France*; and I hoped you'd be joining me."

"Are we going to a wedding or a funeral on the *France*?"

"We can hope for a wedding, maybe a shipboard romance with a chance of lasting once the happy couple gets back to New York. Let's not plan on a funeral. No, Bill, the reason I listed the dark suit and the dress shoes is that there's to be at least one dressy evening during the crossing. Didn't you read the brochure?"

"That one must have fallen through the hole in my brain," I mumbled. Well, Sally was the experienced traveler—and a good thing too.

Almost more than my eagerness to travel, my trepidation, having simmered on the back burner for so many years, had thickened to molasses. From time to time I felt damn near immobilized.

Finally, we got everything we thought we'd need crammed into two large suitcases and three duffel bags. It seemed like more than enough, particularly to the one who would have to muscle the load along the way.

We checked the list and checked it again. We had the travel money, both dollars and pounds. We had letters of introduction from President Burnett to the head librarian at Cambridge University and to several other goodwill organizations he said would be helpful.

And we had our plane tickets, one-way to Heathrow. We planned to book our return on the *France* later on. Each of the girls had a woven green-and-red-striped shoulder bag and some kind of stuffed animal. Suzanne also had a book.

The flight from Pittsburgh to New York was bumpy but otherwise uneventful. For our daughters, it was a first. Rachel thought it was a gas. She spent the whole time manipulating buttons, seats, and trays and drinking more free Coke than she'd ever before been allowed to swallow. She hadn't yet started school, but she was certainly ready for hands-on learning.

No problems? Maybe the fates were trying to get us to drop our guards. The weird ladies went to work full-tilt at Kennedy. A tremendous electrical storm was raging above the airport. We rode the shuttle for what seemed an eternity, missing the British Air stop twice before we tumbled to the fact that its sign was a small-print footnote to Air Canada. Off the shuttle and into line to complete our registration, we ran into trouble with an official-looking type who was frowning at our wet mob. We didn't know what he was exercised about, so Sal showed him our tickets, hoping that would soothe his disposition. He looked at them and worked his frown up to warp level. "Where are your return tickets?" he asked accusingly.

"We haven't booked a return flight," Sally replied. "We intend to return on the *France*, and we'll have plenty of time to arrange that when we get to England."

"Bad idea; the Brits are suspicious of people trying to enter on one-way tickets. They think those outsiders are trying to sneak in and stay to live off the dole. Where are your visas?"

"We were told we didn't need visas to go to England," Sal said. She was doing all the talking: I was silently sweating.

"If you have round-trip tickets showing the date of your return, you don't need visas. What's the reason for your trip—business or pleasure?"

"Well, certainly pleasure, traveling around, seeing the country; but also business, I guess you might say, since my husband has a sabbatical to work in his field."

"A what?"

"A sabbatical. He'll be doing research in the Cambridge University library."

"He's being employed by a library in England? You got a letter from them saying that? The Brits don't like Americans taking their jobs, but if you got a letter hiring him, I guess it'll be OK."

"No, he's not being employed by the library in England. He's an independent scholar who will be doing research on his own project in the university library. We do have a letter from the president of our college to the head librarian of the Cambridge University library." She showed him President Burnett's letter. He looked at it and his frown lessened marginally. "Besides," Sal forged onward: "He won't be making any money; and we'll be spending our money to live there."

"The Brits will like that," he allowed. "That'll probably help, but it would be better if you had a letter from the Cambridge people and visas and return tickets."

I finally found my voice: "So what do we do, book a return flight right now? It isn't what we want to do. Coming home on the *France* is our dream. Besides, we don't know what date to list for the return, and if we use the cash we have for return tickets, what are we going to live on over there?"

Yeah, it was a question; but I didn't expect an answer, and I didn't get one.

"I guess you better go ahead, but you're taking a big chance, buddy. The Brits may send you back here on the next flight."

After that, none of the further rigmarole, including the very personal search, seemed to be much, because I was numb. The girls made it through easily with a minimal wand wave. The official asked Rachel the name of her bear, and she told him, "Plop of Boom."

"Rachel!" Suzanne and Rebecca squealed, "It's Bearie!" But they needn't have been concerned. It was a private joke, and he didn't get it. Maybe it still is.

We were in the economy section of the plane, seated in the middle, five seats in a row. I was in the aisle seat. Soon after we'd belted everyone in, a woman about my age appeared and said, in clipped phrases, "I believe you are sitting in *my* seat," and held her ticket out in front of me.

"Well, madam," I replied, "I believe I'm sitting in *my* seat," and held my ticket up for her to see. It looked like both of us were correct.

A stewardess arrived, looked at both tickets, and said, "Apparently the airline has double-booked this seat." Sally and I and three curious little girls stared at her. The stewardess looked us over. I could almost hear her counting...one, two, three, four, five. "Stay where you are, sir."

I certainly intended to. "Thank you," I said.

The stewardess led the now-glowering woman to the small seat that a stewardess uses during takeoff and landing time. She sat there, very unhappily. I smiled at her. My effort didn't improve her mood. I could almost feel sorry for her, but I'd been through the wringer that day and was running a bit low on magnanimity of soul. When all other passengers were aboard and seated, the stewardess approached the scowling woman and led her forward in the plane out of the economy section. A few minutes later, the stewardess returned and said, "I think the competitor for your seat is happier now in business class."

"Just think, Bill," Sally said, "if you'd given that woman your seat, you could be sitting in business class."

"No thanks, Sal," I replied. "I'd rather be here with you guys. This is *our* adventure."

I woke up because Sally was poking me in the ribs and murmuring, "Bill, Bill, wake up."

"Why, didn't I just go to sleep?"

"No, you've been asleep for hours; and you're snoring like a buzz saw. Besides, we're flying over Ireland. Don't you want to say hello to the land of Yeats and Joyce?"

"That can wait. Right now, I just need some coffee. After a cup or two, I'll look forward to saying hello to the land of Beowulf and Chaucer."

"It won't be long now, and unless I'm dreaming, coffee is on its way. I can smell it!"

Sure enough, the stewardesses were at work reviving their charges with the healing beverage.

"We'll be there in an hour, Bill; are you getting excited?"

"More nervous than excited. I hope they let us in."

"Oh, don't be silly, Bill; look at those three girls of ours. You saw the magic they worked with that stewardess last night. They'd be crazy not to let us in."

But an hour later when we reached the head of the line, passports in hand, I was still nervous. The young official took our passports, gave us the once-over, smiled at the girls, and asked, "How long do you intend to stay in the United Kingdom?"

"A year."

"What is the purpose of your visit?"

"Sabbatical."

Almost before I'd gotten the word out, he began to stamp our passports—*thump! thump! thump!* Then he said, "Welcome to England."

Sally was right. I shouldn't have doubted her instincts. After all, she was the experienced traveler. Still, I had to sit for a while until the *thump, thump, thump* of my heart slowed down. Then we searched for our luggage, a task that had been made easier by the delay. When we finally got to the baggage retrieval area, the more experienced travelers had whipped through there, plucked their bags from the carousel, and made tracks into the larger land. No bags remained on the carousel, and our luggage—three duffels and two large suitcases—had been set off to the side, the only ones waiting to be claimed. They looked like orphans brought in from the storm. We found a cart, loaded it, and began to portage toward the exit. I said to Sally, "I'm going to have to sit down again and get my bearings before I tackle the chore of getting us to Cambridge." Transitions have always taken the wind out of my sails.

Sally took over, saying, "C'mon, Keen girls, let's find an information booth."

"What do we need to know, Mama?" Suzanne asked.

"The best way to get to Cambridge."

That information wasn't going to be necessary, because when we reached the restricted area where the prearranged pickup people were holding up signs with printed names, we spotted John Gatiss. On his shoulders was his little girl, Rachel. She pointed at us and squealed, "There they are, Daddy: there they are!"

Yes, there we were; we were there!

CPSIA information can be obtained
at www.ICGtesting.com
Printed in the USA
BVHW051123300523
665077BV00016B/490